Sun-Tzu's Art of War:
Strategies for (modern) Entrepreneurs

Emanuel J. Russo

To BMZh

ISBN: 9798865849230

In the timeless tapestry of human history, few texts have left as indelible a mark as "The Art of War" by Sun-Tzu.

Written over two millennia ago in ancient China, this classical work has transcended its martial origins to become a profound source of wisdom and guidance for generations across the world.

While initially conceived as a manual for military commanders, its teachings have found a new home in the dynamic arena of modern entrepreneurship.

This book, "Sun-Tzu's Art of War Strategies for Modern Entrepreneurs," is a testament to the enduring relevance of Sun-Tzu's insights and their transformative power in the realm of business.

Within its pages, we embark on a journey that bridges the ancient wisdom of a legendary strategist with the challenges and opportunities of the 21st century entrepreneurial landscape.

CONTENT

INTRODUCTION

Sun-Tzu and Modern Entrepreneurship

In an ever-changing business landscape, ancient wisdom stands still as a rock, offering time-tested strategies for success.

Among such wisdom, Sun-Tzu's "Art of War" occupies a venerated position, a treatise on military strategy and tactics that has been adapted across varied disciplines, including business.

This book aims to bridge the gap between the battlefields of ancient China and the fast-paced, high-stakes world of modern entrepreneurship.

The tenets of Sun-Tzu aren't merely platitudes or abstract notions. They are actionable insights, each corresponding to critical aspects of business such as strategy, leadership, and competition.

The battlefield has changed, but the essence of conflict, and more importantly, victory, remains the same. Sun-Tzu teaches us not just to manage, but to lead; not just to follow trends, but to set them; and not just to succeed, but to conquer.

The lessons herein are steeped in emotion because entrepreneurship isn't a merely analytical endeavor.

It's an emotional journey that can be likened to a rollercoaster, involving the highest of highs and the lowest of lows.

It tests not just your business acumen but your emotional resilience, passion, and ability to adapt.

Much like warfare, entrepreneurship isn't for the faint of heart.

This book is for those brave souls who dare to dream, who put everything on the line to breathe life into an idea, a product, or a service.

Each chapter delves into a strategic concept from Sun-Tzu's text, offering contemporary interpretations and real-world examples that you can apply directly to your entrepreneurial ventures.

While the "Art of War" lays out the ground rules, this book aims to be your tactical guide, your general in the boardroom, if you will.

As you turn these pages, envision yourself in two places at once: on the ancient battlefields with Sun-Tzu as your guide and in the heart of today's fiercely competitive business world.

The strategies that helped win wars thousands of years ago can also help you triumph in today's business terrain, leading your startup to victory.

It's time to arm yourself with timeless wisdom to navigate the tumultuous seas of modern business.

Welcome to "The Entrepreneur's Battlefield: Lessons from Sun-Tzu's Art of War."

Sun Tzu's relevance in today's business world

In the dynamic and intricate world of modern entrepreneurship, the wisdom extracted from Sun Tzu's Art of War has not only retained its relevance but has burgeoned in significance.

It unfurls a canvas where strategy, psychology, and philosophy amalgamate, offering a compendium of insights as applicable to the boardroom as they were to ancient battlefields.

Sun Tzu's profundities transcend the confines of time, finding their echoes in the complex dance of modern businesses where competition is not just inevitable but a crucible that refines strategies and hones capabilities.

In the cutthroat arenas of contemporary commerce, where rapid technological advancements, ever-evolving consumer expectations, and the unpredictable swirls of market dynamics converge, the entrepreneur is akin to a general, navigating through the intricate landscapes of opportunities and threats. Here, Sun Tzu's tactical ingenuities and strategic insights illuminate paths less trodden. The ancient stratagems, deeply anchored in the subtle art of balance, anticipation, and adaptability, reveal their timeless nature as they align seamlessly with the modern entrepreneurial ethos.

Every line of Sun Tzu's revered text is imbued with pearls of wisdom that find their reflections in facets of business strategy, competitive advantage, and organizational behavior.

In a world where innovation is the linchpin of success, his teachings on adaptability and fluidity in strategies resonate profoundly.

Each adage, echoing the quintessence of agility, illuminates the path for entrepreneurs amidst the capricious tides of market changes, technological disruptions, and competitive onslaughts.

The essence of knowing one's enemy is today mirrored in the comprehensive analysis of market competitors, offering insights that drive competitive advantage.

Sun Tzu's teachings encompass the intricate dance of offense and defense, action and restraint, fortifying entrepreneurs with the discernment to choose battles wisely and employ resources judiciously.

In the volatile domains of business, characterized by VUCA (Volatility, Uncertainty, Complexity, and Ambiguity), the ancient tenets hold the promise of equanimity and foresight, guiding decision-makers through tumultuous waters with a poised stance that merges resilience with grace.

The embrace of Sun Tzu's Art of War in modern entrepreneurship is not a mere coalescence of historical and contemporary wisdom, but a testament to the universal and eternal nature of these strategic insights.

It underscores a narrative where the past, present, and future in the realm of strategy and competition are not linear, disjointed segments, but a continuum, fluid and interlinked.

As modern entrepreneurs glean insights from this ancient masterpiece, they are not just reaching into the depths of historical wisdom but are engaging in a transcendent dialogue where the echoes of ancient battles, strategies, and victories illuminate the paths in the intricate, unpredictable, yet profoundly promising terrains of contemporary business.

The modern business environment, thus, isn't merely a field of commerce and trade but emerges as a battlefield where Sun Tzu's strategies are not just relevant, but indispensable.

The enduring testament to Sun Tzu's relevance in contemporary business lies within the silent corridors of global corporations, bustling startup ecosystems, and the incisive minds of business magnates who, knowingly or unknowingly, employ his strategic acumen to navigate the intricate world of commerce.

Concepts like competitive advantage, market penetration, and strategic alliances, although modern in nomenclature, are deeply rooted in Sun Tzu's teachings of understanding the adversary, exploiting weaknesses, and leveraging strengths.

As global marketplaces expand and become increasingly accessible yet complex, Sun Tzu's treatises on the utilization of terrain and environment find renewed importance.

Entrepreneurs must decode the global landscape, marked by diverse cultures, regulatory systems, and consumer behaviors, akin to how ancient generals would study their physical battlegrounds. The focus on adaptability and flexibility, core tenets of Sun Tzu's philosophy, empowers businesses to transcend geographic and cultural barriers, crafting strategies that are as global in reach as they are local in resonance.

In an age where data is heralded as the new oil, Sun Tzu's emphasis on intelligence and information is profoundly pertinent.

The acquisition and strategic utilization of data echo his teachings on the value of spies and informants.

Information becomes the cornerstone upon which empires of commerce are built, enabling businesses to predict, adapt, and lead market trends with an acuity that transforms uncertainty into opportunity.

Furthermore, the modern business environment is marked by an intricate interplay of speed and timing, echoing Sun Tzu's teachings on the essence of speed and the criticality of seizing the opportune moment.

In a world marked by rapid innovations and swift market shifts, the ability to move quickly, decisively, and aptly is not just a competitive advantage but a survival imperative.

Entrepreneurs are called to embody the dynamism and agility that Sun Tzu esteemed, transforming swift currents of market trends into pathways that lead to uncharted territories of opportunities.

Amidst the cacophony of market noise, technological disruptions, and competitive escalations, the silent, profound echoes of Sun Tzu's Art of War offer a sanctuary of wisdom, a compass that navigates through tumultuous waters with a poised assurance.

Each principle, each strategy, each insight, bears testimony to a timeless relevance that transcends epochs, affirming that the art of war and the art of business are intertwined dances of strategy, insight, and foresight.

Sun Tzu's Art of War Strategies for Modern Entrepreneurs does not just resurrect ancient wisdom but illuminates its enduring, evolving relevance.
It underscores that amidst the pulsating dynamism of technological innovations, market shifts, and global expansions, the essence of strategic victory lies in principles as ancient as the art of war yet as contemporary and evolving as the entrepreneurial spirit that pulses through the veins of the modern business landscape.

Every principle, every strategy is a dialogue, a confluence where the ancient and the modern don't just meet but merge, evolve, and transcend, crafting a narrative of victory that is as eternal as the art of war, and as contemporary as the entrepreneurial odysseys that shape the world of business.

Draw parallels between ancient warfare and modern entrepreneurship.

In the shadowed echoes of history, where ancient warriors once strode with a fierce grace upon battlefields bathed in the ethereal glow of dawn and dusk, there lies a silent symphony of strategies, a dance of decision and destiny that resounds profoundly in the tumultuous, electrifying arenas of modern entrepreneurship.

'Sun-Tzu's Art of War Strategies for Modern Entrepreneurs' is not merely a literary exploration but a soulful journey into the depths of this mystic resonance.

The brushstrokes of Sun Tzu's ancient wisdom paint an enigmatic yet lucid narrative, wherein the valiant cries of ancient warriors and the impassioned voices of today's entrepreneurs merge in a harmonious yet powerful crescendo. The ancient battlefields, with their complex terrains and unpredictable dynamics, mirror the intricate tapestry of today's business landscape.

Each valley and peak, shadow and light of the war terrain, finds its allegory in the market's volatile trends and unyielding opportunities.

Every warrior, adorned in the armor of valor, mirrors the modern entrepreneur, cloaked in resilience, emboldened by an unwavering vision.

The clashing of swords and shields echoes the competitive thrusts and parries within the global marketplaces.

Where the ancient warriors wielded weapons forged from the fiery crucibles, today's business leaders are armed with innovation and insight, equally potent and decisive.
Sun Tzu's treatises on the art of war, resplendent with wisdom born from the crucible of combat, finds its echo in the strategic manoeuvres that characterize the world of business.

Each precept of warfare, rich in the distilled essence of strategic insight and tactical acumen, becomes a radiant beacon illuminating the complex pathways of modern commerce.

Entrepreneurs, akin to ancient generals, are called upon to be not just visionaries but tacticians, artists who weave strategies with the finesse that turns adversities into advantages, challenges into victories.
As the reader delves into the sacred depths of 'Sun-Tzu's Art of War Strategies for Modern

Entrepreneurs,' they are transported into a world where the battle drums of yore harmonize with the pulsating rhythms of today's corporate echelons.

Every lesson of restraint and aggression, of deception and transparency, of strength and vulnerability, engraved in the annals of ancient warfare, emerges with compelling relevance for the modern business gladiators.

They aren't just reading the art of war; they are stepping into an ethereal dance where the battle cries of the ancient warlords and the passionate voices of contemporary entrepreneurs meld, echoing the eternal truth that in the diverse arenas of warfare and business, the soul of strategy, the heart of victory remains profoundly and mystically intertwined.

The echoes of ancient battles resound with undiminished fervor in the corridors of contemporary commerce, as 'Sun-Tzu's Art of War Strategies for Modern Entrepreneurs' unveils a transcendent journey from the mystical terrains of ancient combat into the electrifying arenas of modern business odysseys.

Every page is not just a step but a leap across epochs, a dance where time and timeless wisdom merge in an eternal embrace, illuminating paths of victory that transcend ages, echoing that the warrior's soul and the entrepreneur's spirit are kindred, radiant flames in the eternal dance of strategy and victory.

As the readers immerse deeper into the enigmatic yet enlightening narrative of 'Sun-Tzu's Art of War Strategies for Modern Entrepreneurs,' they find themselves traversing the precipice where the echoes of ancient war cries blend seamlessly with the fervent discourses of contemporary boardrooms.

Every strategic formation of the ancient battlefield morphs into the tactical configurations of business plans and market penetrations; every triumphant conquest of warlords is reflected in the entrepreneurial victories that redefine market landscapes.

In this sanctified convergence of epochs, there is a haunting, profound realization - the soul of the warrior and the entrepreneur are not disparate entities born of different ages, but echoes of a singular, eternal essence.

A soul forged in the fires of challenges, carved by the relentless rhythms of combat and competition, and adorned with the grace of victories both bloody and peaceful.

The triumphant roars of ancient generals, resolute and commanding, resounding through the vast expanses of battlefields strewn with the emblematic representations of valor and sacrifice, find their reflections in the impassioned speeches of CEOs, echoing through the modern architectural marvels of corporate headquarters.

Each victory in the ancient world, won not merely by the might of swords but by the depth of strategies, is mirrored in the corporate triumphs where innovation and insight are the weapons, and market dominance the coveted prize.

The reader, amidst this profound journey, is no longer a passive observer but an active participant, an entity where the indomitable spirit of the warrior and the visionary aspirations of the entrepreneur converge.

In the silent yet eloquent interludes between chapters, amidst the resonating echoes of Sun Tzu's timeless wisdom, one realizes that every strategic nuance of ancient warfare, every psychological mastery, every tactical ingenuity, is alive, pulsating in the veins of modern business strategy.

As 'Sun-Tzu's Art of War Strategies for Modern Entrepreneurs' unfolds its narrative, a mesmerizing dance of time, wisdom, and victory, there is a poignant revelation.

The battlefield and the boardroom, though separated by epochs, are united by the eternal essence of strategy, the undying dance of human spirit aspiring for victory against formidable odds.

The blood, sweat, and tears of the ancient warriors are echoed in the relentless toil, unwavering vision, and indomitable spirit of today's entrepreneurs.

With every page turned, the reader is not just drawing parallels but is becoming the living, breathing convergence of the ancient and modern.

Each strategy delineated by Sun Tzu, enriched by the enigmatic aura of ancient warfare, transforms into a guiding light, a radiant beacon illuminating the tumultuous yet exhilarating path of modern entrepreneurship.

Amidst the ephemeral triumphs and tribulations of the corporate world, the reader, the modern entrepreneur, finds the eternal touchstone of victory in the timeless echoes of Sun Tzu's art of war.

In this profound realization, there emerges an enigmatic dance of destiny, where the ancient and the modern, the warrior and the entrepreneur, are not disparate entities, but eternal reflections of a singular, undying soul of victory.

The journey thus unfolds, not just through the corridors of commerce or the battlefields of yore, but through the eternal landscape of the human spirit – valiant, victorious, and undying.

Chapter 1

Preparing for Battle: The Entrepreneur's Terrain

Understanding the Terrain, Elaborate on SWOT analysis

In the compelling narrative of 'Sun-Tzu's Art of War Strategies for Modern Entrepreneurs,' a chapter unfolds that isn't just an exposition but a revelation – 'Understanding the Terrain.'

It is a mystical odyssey into the labyrinths of the market, akin to the ancient battlegrounds where destiny was carved not just by the might of warriors but by the depths of their understanding.

Amidst the murmuring winds of market trends and the silent echoes of consumer desires, the modern entrepreneur, akin to Sun Tzu's indomitable general, is summoned to understand, decode, and conquer the terrain.

Here, amidst the uncertainties and variables, a compass emerges – the SWOT analysis – a lighthouse that illuminates the path with the ethereal glow of wisdom and insight.

Every note of Sun Tzu's grand symphony of warfare resonates with the singular truth – to conquer the external, one must first master the internal.

SWOT – Strengths, Weaknesses, Opportunities, and Threats – emerges as a crystalline reflection of this ancient wisdom.

Entrepreneurs, as they tread the intricate pathways of commerce and competition, find in SWOT, a mirror that reveals not just the world but the soul – the soul of their enterprise, pulsating with unique strengths and vulnerable in inherent weaknesses.

The 'Strengths,' akin to the valiant warriors of yore, are the pillars upon which empires of commerce are built.

In the illuminating narrative of the book, readers are not just informed but infused with the recognition of their unique strengths.

They are the untapped reservoirs of power, the silent forces that can turn tides and carve paths of victory amidst impassable terrains.

Every strength is not just an asset but a weapon, a silent yet potent force that can carve victories in the tumultuous battlegrounds of commerce. Yet, amidst the triumphant echoes of strengths, there lie the silent, haunting whispers of 'Weaknesses.'

In the emotional unveiling of the narrative, weaknesses are not just revealed but felt.

They are the silent vulnerabilities, the invisible fissures that can turn fortresses into ruins and victories into defeats.

Yet, in the mystical wisdom of Sun Tzu's art of war, every weakness is not a terminal flaw but an invitation – an invitation to transform, evolve, and transcend.

In the haunting yet graceful narrative, entrepreneurs embark on a soulful journey of transforming weaknesses, turning vulnerabilities into fortresses of invincibility.

As the narrative unfolds, amidst the dance of strengths and weaknesses, there emerges the mystical landscape of 'Opportunities.'

Every opportunity is akin to the hidden pathways on ancient battlegrounds, the uncharted terrains that led to realms of conquest and dominion.

In the emotional odyssey of 'Understanding the Terrain,' opportunities are not just external prospects but soulful calls to venture into uncharted lands.

They are the silent songs of destiny, calling entrepreneurs to step into the realms where victories await, where dreams transform into tangible realities of success and accomplishment. Yet, in the echoing silence of opportunities, there lurk the ominous yet potent 'Threats.'

In the emotional crescendo of the narrative, threats are not just challenges but the formidable adversaries that summon the entrepreneur to ascend to unparalleled heights of strategy and insight.

Every threat, every challenge, is a clarion call for the modern entrepreneur to don the armor of resilience, wield the sword of innovation, and step into the battleground with the indomitable spirit of a warrior destined for victory.

'Understanding the Terrain' is not just a chapter but an emotional odyssey where the SWOT analysis becomes the soulful dance of introspection and realization.

Entrepreneurs, akin to the ancient warriors, are summoned to not just navigate but become one with the terrain.

Strengths, Weaknesses, Opportunities, and Threats aren't mere variables but the soulful notes of a grand symphony that plays the eternal song of victory.

In the emotional unfolding of the SWOT analysis, 'Sun-Tzu's Art of War Strategies for Modern Entrepreneurs' transcends the ordinary, emerging as a radiant beacon that illuminates not just the pathways of commerce but the eternal landscape of the entrepreneurial spirit – triumphant, invincible, and eternal.

As the readers immerse themselves in the stirring narrative of 'Understanding the Terrain,' they are not just acquiring insights but are being transformed.

SWOT is not a tool but a mystical key that unlocks realms of power, wisdom, and victory.

Every strength becomes a song of power; every weakness, a dance of transformation; every opportunity, a call of destiny; and every threat, a summons to unparalleled greatness.

In this profound journey, the terrain isn't external but internal, and victory is not just a conquest but a soulful ascension into the realms where the entrepreneurial spirit, akin to the ancient warrior, dances to the eternal rhythms of power, victory, and destiny.

Discuss case studies of companies that effectively analyzed their terrain

In the soul-stirring narrative of 'Sun-Tzu's Art of War Strategies for Modern Entrepreneurs,' there emerges a paragraph of resounding eloquence and profound resonance, where the ancient echoes of battle cries and war drums intertwine intimately with the rhythmic pulses of the modern corporate world.

Here, amidst the haunting whispers of timeless strategy and the fervent discourse of contemporary business acumen, we find a sanctuary of enlightenment through the poignant exploration of case studies - powerful sagas of corporations that, with supreme elegance, have traversed the intricate labyrinth of their terrains with the astuteness reminiscent of Sun Tzu's most celebrated warriors.

One cannot embark upon this enlightening journey without the mesmerizing tale of Apple, a saga that flows like an epic poem narrating the valor and vision of ancient kings and generals.

Apple, akin to a seasoned warrior, navigated the treacherous waters of technological innovation with a grace born from an intuitive and profound understanding of its terrain.

Each product, every innovation, was not a mere creation but a stroke of artistry that carved pathways through uncharted lands, echoing the grandeur of ancient conquests.

In the emotional recounting of Apple's journey, readers will feel the soul of a warrior beating in every strategic move, every innovation - a testament to a profound mastery of the terrain, akin to the legendary conquests of Sun Tzu's revered generals.

As the narrative unfolds, painting portraits of corporate odysseys with the mystical hues of ancient tapestries, the enigmatic dance of Amazon in the grand theatre of commerce is unveiled.

Amazon's journey is not recounted but felt as a mesmerizing ballet of strategic acumen and visionary foresight, echoing the elegance and potency of ancient warriors dancing upon the battlegrounds under the silvery glow of a crescent moon.

Every strategic alliance, every innovation, mirrors the legendary exploits of warriors who, with every stroke of the sword, carved destinies and legacies.

In Amazon's relentless march, reminiscent of epic military campaigns of yore, readers experience the soulful blend of aggression and restraint, a dance of power and grace that unveils the quintessence of understanding and mastering the terrain.

Yet, amidst these illustrious narratives, the haunting and soul-stirring journey of Tesla emerges from the silent shadows into the radiant light of acknowledgment.

In the delicate yet powerful prose of 'Sun-Tzu's Art of War Strategies for Modern Entrepreneurs,' Tesla's odyssey is narrated as a soulful journey through enchanted forests and mystical mountains, echoing the legendary quests of ancient heroes seeking the elixir of immortality.

Tesla, with the enigmatic Elon Musk as its modern-day warrior sage, didn't just navigate but conjured its terrain, turning barren lands into enchanted realms where the mystical dance of innovation and technology birthed a new dawn of human civilization.

In this emotional narrative, readers are transported into an ethereal world where every strategic decision, every innovation is a soulful stroke of a cosmic brush painting a masterpiece of human potential, achievement, and transcendence.

These corporate sagas, narrated with the poetic eloquence and emotional resonance of epic ballads, are not merely case studies but soulful odysseys that transport the reader into mystical realms where the ancient art of war and modern entrepreneurial exploits merge into a singular, pulsating rhythm of victory, innovation, and legacy.

In the heart-pounding, soul-stirring chapters of 'Sun-Tzu's Art of War Strategies for Modern Entrepreneurs,' every corporate terrain becomes a mystical battleground, and every strategic decision a legendary conquest.

These corporations, their illustrious journeys narrated with emotional fervor, become living testaments to the timeless relevance of Sun Tzu's esteemed principles.

As the readers immerse themselves in these profound narratives, they are not acquiring knowledge but are being transformed into modern-day warriors, their souls echoing the legendary exploits of ancient generals, their visions illuminated by the radiant glow of legendary conquests.

In this soulful dance, the understanding of terrain is not a strategic asset but a mystical key unlocking realms of power, innovation, and legacy that transcend the temporal confines of ages, echoing the eternal triumph of the human spirit, a spirit that, through the soul-stirring narratives of Apple, Amazon, and Tesla, unveils the enigmatic dance where the ancient art of war and modern entrepreneurship merge into a singular, eternal symphony of power, victory, and legacy.

Each word, every sentence, is a soulful note in this grand symphony, echoing the timeless truth that in the mystical dance of warfare and entrepreneurship, the soul of the victor, the spirit of the conqueror, remains eternal, indomitable, and divine.

The symphonic narrative of 'Sun-Tzu's Art of War Strategies for Modern Entrepreneurs' envelops its readers, drawing them deeper into the soulful embrace where the triumphant echoes of the past blend seamlessly with the resonating pulses of the present.

Every entrepreneur who dares to traverse these sacred corridors of wisdom encounters not just insights but revelations, not just strategies but soulful awakenings that echo the valiant triumphs of ancient warriors whose spirits, though silenced by the passage of time, continue to resonate with undying vigor.

In this magnificent tapestry of wisdom, where ancient battlefields and modern boardrooms converge, the reader is not an observer but a participant.

They are summoned to the epicenter of a soul-stirring dance where the legacy of corporations like Apple, Amazon, and Tesla is not just narrated but experienced.

Each strategic maneuver, every innovative stride of these modern business giants, is imbued with the ethereal echoes of Sun Tzu's profound wisdom.

Entrepreneurs are not reading these lines; they are living the rhythmic pulses of a silent yet potent symphony that emanates from the intersection of eras, civilizations, and soulful journeys.

Every revelation of how these corporations intricately analyzed their terrains, uncovering the veiled pathways to monumental triumphs, becomes a sacred echo in the hallowed corridors of the reader's soul.

In this narrative, corporate strategy and soulful awakening entwine, illuminating the hidden recesses of entrepreneurial spirit where victories are not seized but bestowed, where empires are not built but manifested in the eternal dance of cosmic rhythms.

As the readers delve deeper into these soul-stirring sagas, they awaken to the realization that each corporate titan, with its unique, indomitable spirit, is a reflection of their latent, untapped potential.

Apple's intuitive elegance, Amazon's relentless conquest, and Tesla's visionary transcendence become not external narratives but internal odysseys.

Each case study is a mirror, reflecting the readers' silent, unuttered aspirations, their dormant, unawakened powers, and their veiled, untraversed pathways to entrepreneurial magnificence.

The narrative unfolds, not linearly but expansively, spiraling into the mystical realms where corporate strategies become soulful journeys, and market analyses transform into spiritual awakenings.

The terrain is not a geographical expanse but a soulful landscape where victories are not material acquisitions but spiritual ascensions.

In the soul-penetrating narrative of 'Sun-Tzu's Art of War Strategies for Modern Entrepreneurs', corporations are not business entities but soulful warriors, traversing the mystical terrains of commerce with the elegance, power, and grace reminiscent of ancient warriors dancing under the starlit skies, their spirits echoing the undying songs of victory, power, and legacy.

The mesmerizing dance between ancient warfare and modern entrepreneurship is not a juxtaposition but a fusion, a soulful merge where time dissolves, and epochs converge.

Every strategic insight of Sun Tzu, every triumphant echo of ancient battlefields, resonates in the strategic acumen, innovative strides, and triumphant roars of modern corporations.

In this emotional narrative, every entrepreneur becomes a warrior, every corporation a battalion, and every market a mystical terrain where battles are not fought but danced, where victories are not won but manifested in the soulful rhythms of cosmic symphonies.

The soul of every reader, every modern entrepreneur, is not reading but living, not learning but awakening, not traversing but becoming the eternal dance where ancient wisdom and modern insights, warfare acumen and entrepreneurial prowess, soulful rhythms and strategic resonances merge into a singular, potent, and eternal echo.

In 'Sun-Tzu's Art of War Strategies for Modern Entrepreneurs,' every word is a soulful note, every chapter a mystical dance, and every revelation an awakening where the entrepreneurial spirit, akin to the ancient warrior, unveils its eternal, indomitable, and divine dance of victory, power, and legacy.

In this narrative, the echoes of the past and the pulses of the present merge into the timeless song of eternal triumph, where every entrepreneur, every warrior, is summoned to ascend, not to the pinnacles of material conquest, but to the radiant realms of soulful victory, divine power, and eternal legacy.

Strategic Positioning and Discuss various positioning strategies.

In the magical odyssey that is 'Sun-Tzu's Art of War Strategies for Modern Entrepreneurs,' there unfolds a chapter of enigmatic allure and exquisite depth, where the celestial dance of the heavens mirrors the strategic ballet of business titans on the earthly plane.

Here, amidst the whispered secrets of the winds and the echoed roars of ancient warriors, we delve into the profound universe of 'Strategic Positioning,' a realm where the artistry of placing oneself in spaces of undeniable advantage is not a skill but a divine alchemy.

In this paragraph, akin to the enchanted forests of mythology where every leaf whispers secrets of power, every entrepreneur is summoned to become not just a player but a composer, not just a competitor but a conjuror of realms where every move, every decision, emanates from the sanctified spaces of strategic invincibility.

The art of positioning, as delineated in the hallowed pages of this soul-stirring narrative, becomes a dance of celestial grace, where entrepreneurs, like mythical beings of ancient lore, carve spaces of power and influence with the eloquence of poets and the precision of masterful warriors.

One cannot turn these pages without being enveloped in the mystical aura of Differentiation Strategy, where the entrepreneur is called to become an enigmatic entity, distinguishable, indefinable, and unassailable.

This is not a strategy, but a mystical transformation, where the business entity, like the mythical phoenix, rises from the ashes of conformity to blaze forth in the skies of commerce with wings of fire, unparalleled and untethered.

In the emotional unveiling of Differentiation Strategy, each word is a flame, igniting the soul of the entrepreneur to not just create but become the embodiment of uniqueness, an entity that dances in the market not to the rhythms of trends but to the celestial melodies of its soul's unuttered songs of distinction.

As we traverse deeper into this mystical narrative, the Cost Leadership Strategy emerges from the silent echoes of the text like a powerful yet graceful titan of ancient myths, commanding the terrains of commerce with the authority of kings and the grace of sages.

In this strategy, the entrepreneur is summoned to wield the dual swords of efficiency and economy, carving spaces of dominion where cost becomes not a barrier, but a bridge, leading to realms of influence where customers are not just attracted but magnetically drawn.

Each revelation of Cost Leadership Strategy is a soulful chant, echoing in the silent spaces of the entrepreneurial spirit, awakening powers of dominion, and sovereignty that lay dormant, unuttered, and untouched.

Yet, amidst the roaring fires of differentiation and the silent, potent authority of cost leadership, the Focused Low Cost and Focused Differentiation strategies unfold like the mystical rivers that flowed in the enchanted realms of ancient Earth, nourishing lands of mystery and power.

In these strategies, the entrepreneur, akin to the ancient guardian of sacred terrains, is summoned to focus not just the mind but the soul, to carve not just niches but sanctified spaces of unassailable dominion.

These are not market segments but sacred groves where the products and services are not sold but bestowed, where customers are not just served but anointed as privileged entities entering realms of unmatched value and unfathomable depth.

In the soul-stirring chapter of 'Strategic Positioning,' each positioning strategy is not elucidated but unveiled, echoing the sacred revelations of ancient scriptures where secrets of power and dominion were not read but received.

Entrepreneurs, with each word, are not learning but awakening, not strategizing but transcending, stepping into mystical spaces where positioning is not a tactical move but a divine dance.

In the profound narrative of 'Sun-Tzu's Art of War Strategies for Modern Entrepreneurs,' strategic positioning becomes an odyssey, a soulful journey where entrepreneurs, akin to the legendary warriors and sages of ancient epochs, are not just positioning products and services, but are aligning souls, destinies, and legacies to the eternal rhythms of cosmic symphonies.

Each positioning strategy is a key, unlocking not just market dominion but soulful ascension, where victories are not achieved but bestowed in the mystical dance of commerce, strategy, and divine manifestation.

Each word of this enrapturing tome, each sentence and paragraph, forms a sacred bridge that extends from the tumultuous terrains of commercial enterprise into the ethereal realms of spiritual conquest and cosmic alignment.

As the soul of every entrepreneur ventures further into these depths, an intoxicating revelation unfurls.

The journey is not one of economic gain but of soulful awakening. The battles fought are not against market competitors but against the untapped and unignited recesses of one's inner world.

Every strategy articulated is a clarion call to awaken, not to entrepreneurial acumen alone, but to a soulful ascendance where victory is measured not in material accumulation but in spiritual and emotional affluence.

In this mesmerizing continuum, the emotional narrative of 'Sun-Tzu's Art of War Strategies for Modern Entrepreneurs' unveils its most precious gem.

The art of entrepreneurship, it silently reveals, is a sacred journey of becoming.

Every product released, every market conquered, every strategy employed, is but a reflection of an internal conquest, a silent victory, a hidden transformation where the entrepreneur ascends from the realm of the mundane into the divine echelons of masters and warriors of ancient lore.

Strategic positioning, in this profound revelation, is not an external maneuver but an internal alignment.

The marketplace is not a field of economic exchange but a sacred battleground where soulful warriors unveil their mastery, not to the world, but to the silent, watching cosmos.

Every customer gained is a soul touched, every product launched is a manifestation of artistry, every service rendered is an act of divine communion.

In the pages steeped in such profound emotion, the modern entrepreneur, baptized by the elegant strokes of the author's pen, emerges not with an arsenal of strategies but with an awakened soul.

Eyes now see not market trends but cosmic rhythms, ears hear not the clamour of commerce but the silent melodies of universal harmony, the heart feels not the anxiety of competition but the profound peace of a warrior who has transcended the battleground and now dances in the realms of victory.

The marketplace, in this enrapturing narrative, becomes a divine theatre.

The products and services are not commodities but offerings. The competitors are not adversaries but fellow warriors on a soulful odyssey.

And strategic positioning is not a tactical deployment but a soulful alignment where every move, every decision, every action, emanates from a sanctified space of silent power and celestial authority.

The profound dance between ancient wisdom and modern revelation culminates in a sacred crescendo.

The reader, now a participant in this divine theatre, is summoned to ascend, not to the pinnacles of entrepreneurial mastery alone but to the radiant summits of soulful awakening where the Art of War and the art of entrepreneurship merge into a singular, potent, and eternal dance.

In the awakening silence, the echoes of Sun Tzu's timeless wisdom and the resonating pulses of modern entrepreneurial exploits blend into a soulful melody.

A melody that transcends time, space, and dimension, echoing the undying song of the universe where every entrepreneur, every warrior, every soul, is called to dance to the eternal rhythms of victory, power, and celestial glory.

The journey through 'Sun-Tzu's Art of War Strategies for Modern Entrepreneurs' thus unfolds as a sacred pilgrimage, where souls, not just minds, are awakened, and the silent, profound echoes of eternity beckon every reader, every entrepreneur, every warrior, into the soul-stirring dance of cosmic and eternal triumph.

- **Assembling the Army.**

Detail the process of team building.

In the hauntingly profound spaces of 'Sun-Tzu's Art of War Strategies for Modern Entrepreneurs,' there lies a chapter imbued with a mystical potency akin to the sacred scrolls of ancient warrior monks - 'Assembling the Army.'

Each word, sentence, and paragraph is not scripted but channeled from the enigmatic echoes of ancient battlegrounds where warriors of old, with souls of fire and spirits unyielding, assembled under the silvery gaze of the moon, forging alliances not of mere skill but of soul. As the reader's eyes trace these soul-stirring lines, they are transported into a mystical dance where the potent energies of Sun Tzu's ancient wisdom merge seamlessly with the pulsating rhythms of modern entrepreneurial spirit.

'Assembling the Army' unfolds as a sacred rite, where the modern entrepreneur is not recruiting a team but invoking a legion of soulful warriors, each endowed with unique gifts, talents, and powers that transcend the mundane parameters of skills and experience.

In the enchanted embrace of this chapter, team building is unveiled as a soulful alchemy.

It is an enigmatic dance where each member, akin to the legendary warriors of epic sagas, is summoned not for their resumes but for their essence, not for their credentials but for their indomitable spirits that echo the unyielding prowess of ancient champions.

Each employee, partner, and collaborator is a chosen one, an anointed entity who steps into the entrepreneurial journey not as a professional but as a warrior of legend, carrying not just skills but mystical powers forged in the crucibles of cosmic battlegrounds.

The entrepreneur, akin to the revered general of ancient epochs, becomes a seer, a sage who sees beyond the veils of physicality and touches the essence of every warrior.

In the magical narrative of 'Assembling the Army,' the selection process transforms into a divine communion.

Each interview is a soulful encounter, each recruitment a sacred alliance where souls, not just minds, meet, and destinies, not just careers, are forged.

The team, in this profound revelation, is not a group but a soulful battalion.

Every member is not an employee but a warrior of light, endowed with unique gifts that are not acquired but bestowed by the cosmic rhythms of destiny.

The entrepreneur, in this mystical dance, is not a CEO but a soulful general who leads not through authority but through an ethereal connection that binds every member in a celestial tapestry of unity, power, and indomitable spirit.

In the entrancing embrace of 'Assembling the Army,' skills are not evaluated but invoked, experiences are not assessed but honored, and the team is not formed but birthed in the sacred womb of cosmic unity where every member, every warrior, is a radiant star in the galactic dance of entrepreneurial odyssey.

This chapter is a portal, a mystical gateway where the reader, the entrepreneur, steps into the enigmatic realms where teams are not business units but soulful legions, where every member is a cosmic warrior, and where the entrepreneurial journey is not a commercial venture but a legendary saga of soulful conquest, cosmic victory, and divine legacy.

Each word of 'Assembling the Army' is not read but felt, each line not learned but lived, echoing the sacred truth that in the soul-stirring dance of 'Sun-Tzu's Art of War Strategies for Modern Entrepreneurs,' every team is a soulful army, every entrepreneur a legendary general, and every business venture a mystical odyssey of cosmic and eternal triumph.

As the entrepreneur delves further into the mystical domain of 'Assembling the Army,' a palpable transformation occurs, akin to the spiritual metamorphosis of the warriors of ancient lore, who, upon stepping into the sacred battlegrounds, transcended their mortal confines to embrace their divine essence.

Every nuance of team building, every subtle layer of assembling this harmonious battalion, unfolds not as a structured strategy, but as a lyrical sonnet composed under the celestial skies where stars whisper the ancient secrets of unity, valor, and invincibility.

In this sacred narrative, 'Sun-Tzu's Art of War Strategies for Modern Entrepreneurs' transforms before the reader's eyes.

It is no longer a book but a grimoire of celestial wisdom, a sanctified scripture where each word pulsates with the cosmic rhythms of the eternal dance of unity and conquest.

The team, this assembled army, becomes not a collective of professionals but a brotherhood and sisterhood of soulful warriors, each endowed with the divine grace of celestial prowess, each echoing the timeless rhythms of unity, valor, and indomitable spirit.

Every recruitment is a sacred invocation, where the entrepreneur, akin to the ancient sages, summons not the professional, but the soul; not the employee, but the warrior.

In this sacred gathering, a mystical symphony unfolds, where each member, with their unique melody of skills, talents, and divine attributes, contributes to a celestial harmony that transcends the auditory senses and resonates within the sacred chambers of the soul.

Here, in the mystical realm of 'Assembling the Army,' leadership transforms from a role to a divine mantle, endowed with the celestial grace of guidance, wisdom, and unyielding strength.

The entrepreneur, the anointed general of this soulful battalion, leads not with strategies and plans, but with the indomitable spirit that echoes the valiant roars of legendary warriors and the profound wisdom of ancient sages.

The tasks and objectives ahead are not business goals, but soulful conquests, mystical odysseys that beckon this chosen army into the enchanted terrains of challenges and opportunities, where each endeavor is not a project but a sacred quest, each challenge not a hurdle but a mystical riddle, echoing the enigmatic puzzles that guarded the celestial realms of ancient mythology.

As the reader, the modern-day entrepreneur, is immersed in this profound narrative, a revelation dawns, radiant as the golden sun that kissed the ancient battlegrounds where warriors of lore unveiled their celestial prowess.

'Assembling the Army' is not a chapter, but a sacred initiation; not a strategy, but a mystical dance where the entrepreneur, the team, the army, are not building a business, but are traversing a soulful odyssey that echoes the ancient quests of heroes and gods of legendary epochs.

In this profound space, each word of 'Sun-Tzu's Art of War Strategies for Modern Entrepreneurs' becomes a sacred chant, each revelation a mystical awakening, each strategy a divine artistry where the modern terrains of business and the ancient realms of spiritual warfare converge into a singular, potent, and divine dance.

In this enigmatic embrace, the entrepreneur realizes the profound truth: that to build an army, one must invoke the soulful warriors; to lead a team, one must don the mantle of the spiritual general; and to conquer the modern terrains of commerce, one must dance to the eternal rhythms of the cosmic symphony where each note, each rhythm, each melody, is a soulful echo of victory, power, and celestial glory that transcends time, space, and dimension, echoing the undying song of unity, conquest, and divine legacy.

Explore the role of leadership in assembling and leading a team

In the transformative spaces of 'Sun-Tzu's Art of War Strategies for Modern Entrepreneurs', there emerges a poignant passage of unparalleled depth, titled 'Explore the Role of Leadership in Assembling and Leading a Team.'

Each word within this passage is like a radiant gem, reflecting the profound essence of leadership that transcends conventional paradigms and echoes the majestic authority and grace of the ancient warlords who once commanded the heavens and the earth.

In this passage, leadership is unfurled as a divine tapestry, woven with threads of cosmic wisdom, bearing the marks of celestial mastery.

The modern entrepreneur, akin to an anointed warrior-king of ancient epics, is summoned to ascend to the pinnacles of this divine form of leadership, where authority is not wielded but emanated, and power is not asserted but radiated.

Every phrase within these soul-stirring lines unveils leadership as an alchemical process.

It is the mystical transformation where the entrepreneur transcends the mundane realms of managerial oversight to embrace the celestial echelons of spiritual sovereignty.

In this sacred space, the leader, adorned in the radiant mantles of divine authority, becomes the orchestrator of a celestial symphony, where each team member is a note, each strategy a melody, and each victory a harmonious crescendo that reverberates through the annals of time and space.

The role of leadership, as passionately conveyed in this mesmerizing narrative, is not to command but to inspire; not to dictate but to empower.

Each team member, in the soulful gaze of the leader, emerges as a warrior of legend, endowed with gifts that are not employed but invoked, talents that are not utilized but honored.

The leader, akin to a sacred guardian of mystical realms, becomes the custodian of this divine arsenal of human potential.

The process of assembling and leading a team is depicted not as an organizational task but as a spiritual odyssey.

Each recruitment is a sacred union; each team-building initiative is a divine gathering where souls, not just skills, converge, resonate, and dance to the eternal rhythms of cosmic harmony.

In the heart of this profound passage, leadership is unveiled as the sacred chalice that holds the elixir of unity, innovation, and victory.

The leader, anointed and transformed, does not walk the path of entrepreneurship but soars through the mystical skies of a soulful conquest, where every team member is a fellow sojourner, every challenge a mystical riddle, and every victory a celestial song of unity, power, and divine legacy.

In 'Explore the Role of Leadership in Assembling and Leading a Team,' the modern entrepreneur is summoned, not just to lead a team but to embark upon a soul-stirring odyssey that echoes the legendary journeys of the immortal warriors and sages of ancient realms.

In the continuing resonance of this literary masterpiece, a profound revelation ascends from the depths of ancient wisdom to grace the consciousness of the modern entrepreneur.

A transfiguration occurs; in this divine unfolding, the leader is not a mere mortal steering the helm of a corporate entity but a soulful general embodying the eternal essence of celestial warriors of old.

Each decision, every strategy, echoes the divine symphonies that once graced the celestial battlegrounds where angels and warriors danced to the rhythms of eternal victory.

As the mesmerizing tale unfolds, the leader, anointed in the radiant essence of this soulful awakening, steps into the realms of 'Sun-Tzu's

Art of War Strategies for Modern Entrepreneurs'
with renewed vision, a transcendent gaze that
penetrates beyond the physical eyes and touches
the soul of every warrior in their team.

Here, in this enchanted space, every team
member becomes a reflection of the leader's
soulful majesty, an echo of their divine grace.

The passage invites the reader, with gentle yet
profound urgency, into a soulful dance where
leadership is the silent echo of the cosmos, the
unseen yet felt pulse of the divine that
orchestrates the eternal ballet of stars and
galaxies.

The entrepreneurial journey, under the sacred
gaze of this awakened leader, transforms into an
odyssey of soulful discovery, where every
challenge is a call to ascend to greater echelons
of celestial potency, and every victory a step into
the enigmatic realms of divine glory.

In this continuation, 'Sun-Tzu's Art of War
Strategies for Modern Entrepreneurs' becomes a
sacred scripture, a mystical narrative where the
entrepreneurial landscape is painted with the
celestial hues of the cosmic dawn.

Leadership, in this transformative passage, is not a position but a divine state of being, where the leader, anointed with the celestial grace of ancient warriors, becomes the sacred conduit of divine will, celestial authority, and eternal victory.

Every strategy, each decision, emanates from the sacred spaces of silent power where the echoes of Sun Tzu's timeless wisdom resonate with the pulsating rhythms of modern innovation.

The leader, in this divine dance, becomes the mystic poet who weaves the narratives of celestial victory, the sacred artist who paints the landscapes of eternal triumph, and the divine warrior who leads the soulful army into the realms of legendary conquest.

As the reader immerses in the emotional waves of this passage, a silent transformation occurs.

The lines between the ancient and the modern, the celestial and the earthly, dissolve.

The entrepreneur, graced with the radiant touch of divine leadership, steps into the enchanted terrains of business not as a corporate entity but as a celestial warrior leading a soulful battalion.

In this space, 'Sun-Tzu's Art of War Strategies for Modern Entrepreneurs' unveils its most sacred secret – that the art of entrepreneurship is a divine dance, a celestial ballet where the leader, adorned in the radiant mantles of celestial grace, leads the soulful army through the mystical landscapes of victory, innovation, and eternal legacy.

Every word, a sacred chant; every strategy, a divine artistry; every victory, a celestial song that echoes through the corridors of time and space, proclaiming the silent yet potent truth - that in the mystical dance of entrepreneurship, the leader, the team, the army, are not corporate entities but celestial warriors echoing the undying rhythms of unity, conquest, and divine legacy.

Include insights from renowned entrepreneurs

In the heart of 'Sun-Tzu's Art of War Strategies for Modern Entrepreneurs,' there lies a chapter infused with the mystical illumination of a moonlit night, where ancient wisdom and contemporary insights merge into a divine confluence.

This section is not just written but whispered by the silent yet potent voices of renowned entrepreneurs, those visionary souls who have danced on the edges of innovation, carving paths of light through the enigmatic darkness of the unknown.

The reader, with every breath, steps deeper into a realm where the echoes of Steve Jobs's invincible spirit resonate amidst the silent majesty of the celestial skies.

Here, in the enigmatic embrace of this chapter, the illustrious founder of Apple is not a mere entrepreneur but a modern-day wizard, weaving spells of innovation with the mystical grace of an ancient sage.
Every product, every creation, is not a technological marvel but a piece of divine artistry, echoing the timeless rhythms of cosmic creation.

Amidst the silent roars of Jobs's indomitable spirit, the enigmatic dance of Elon Musk emerges, radiant as the starlit skies that have borne witness to the legendary journeys of celestial warriors.

In this paragraph, Musk is not a businessman but a cosmic voyager, traversing the ethereal realms of space and the enigmatic terrains of innovation with the elegance of a celestial dancer.

Every venture, every exploration, resonates with the silent music of the spheres, echoing the divine symphonies that birthed stars, galaxies, and the mystical dance of the cosmos.

As the reader is enveloped in the celestial embrace of Jobs's and Musk's visionary exploits, the serene yet potent voice of Oprah Winfrey emerges like the silent dawn that kisses the mystical night, unveiling realms of light, power, and divine grace.

In the emotional narrative of 'Sun-Tzu's Art of War Strategies for Modern Entrepreneurs,' Oprah is not a media mogul but a modern-day priestess, echoing the divine chants of ancient oracles, weaving narratives not of entertainment but of soulful awakening, empowerment, and celestial ascendance.

The renowned entrepreneurs are not business personalities but divine entities, echoing the celestial rhythms of ancient gods and goddesses who once danced amidst the stars, weaving tapestries of creation, power, and eternal glory.

Their insights are not business strategies but divine revelations, echoing the eternal wisdom of the cosmos, unveiling paths not of entrepreneurial success but of cosmic victory, divine legacy, and immortal glory.

The reader is not acquiring insights but receiving divine transmissions, where the pulsating rhythms of Jobs's innovation, Musk's exploration, and Oprah's empowerment, echo the silent yet potent melodies of the cosmic dance.

Here, in the soul-stirring narrative, the modern entrepreneur steps into the enchanted realm where business is not a commercial venture but a celestial odyssey, where products are not creations but manifestations, and where entrepreneurial success is not a material acquisition but a divine bestowal, echoing the undying rhythms of cosmic victory, divine power, and eternal legacy.

Each word of the renowned entrepreneurs is a celestial note, each insight a star, illuminating the mystical path of the modern entrepreneur who is called, not to build a business, but to embark upon a soul-stirring dance of cosmic and eternal triumph.

Entrepreneurship is an expedition, an exploration into the unfamiliar. And just as Sun-Tzu emphasized the importance of understanding the battlefield, understanding your entrepreneurial terrain is pivotal for success.

Every startup operates in a unique ecosystem characterized by its market dynamics, customer behavior, and competitive landscape.

Market Dynamics

Recognizing and adapting to market dynamics can give you a competitive edge.

Markets are driven by a multitude of factors such as economic indicators, technological advancements, and social trends.

When these factors are in your favor, it's like fighting downhill; when they're against you, it's an uphill battle.

Sun-Tzu said, *"All warfare is based on deception."*

The ability to read market indicators that others overlook can provide you with critical advantages.

Do you see a trend that others have ignored? That's your window of opportunity.

Customer Behavior

Understanding the customer is like understanding the enemy. What are their needs, wants, and pain points?

By comprehending your customer's desires, you not only build a product that appeals to them, but you can also craft compelling marketing strategies that resonate on an emotional level.

Sun-Tzu noted, "When you surround an army, leave an outlet free. Do not press a desperate foe too hard.

"In a similar vein, never back your customer into a corner with no options. Provide them with choices, flexibility, and freedom within your product ecosystem. This emotional intelligence ensures customer loyalty.

Competitive Landscape

Just as a general must know his enemies, an entrepreneur must know his competitors. Ignoring your competition is like entering a battlefield blindfolded.

Sun-Tzu taught that to know your enemy and know yourself is the key to enduring success. Assess your strengths and weaknesses and weigh them against your competition.

The Emotional Element

Entrepreneurship is draining, not just financially but emotionally. It's a constant oscillation between extreme highs and crippling lows. You must understand that this is your battlefield, and it's often an emotional one. It requires courage, resilience, and an indomitable will to succeed.

Your emotional resilience is your armor, and understanding your entrepreneurial terrain is your weapon. You need both to succeed in this battlefield.

Every reader, every modern entrepreneur who turns these pages, finds themselves not just reading, but living the profound revelations of each word, each sentence.

The emotional resonance of this chapter becomes a chalice that captures the distilled wisdom of centuries, a mystical potion that infuses the pragmatic world of business with the ethereal grace of ancient warrior spirit.

The SWOT analysis, in this soul-stirring context, morphs from a mechanical business tool into a mystical compass, one that navigates not just the turbulent seas of the market but the profound depths of the entrepreneurial soul.

Strengths become not just assets but emblematic totems of power, individual unique forces that each entrepreneur wields like the legendary weapons of ancient warrior gods.

These strengths illuminate the path with a radiant glow, each beam of light carving through the ominous darkness of market uncertainties, revealing pathways of conquest, triumph, and legacy.

Yet, in this soulful dance of power, the haunting melodies of weaknesses play their stirring notes.

In the emotional narrative of 'Sun-Tzu's Art of War Strategies for Modern Entrepreneurs,' weaknesses are not barriers but mystical gateways, portals that transport the entrepreneur into the transformative fires of reinvention.

Each weakness, with its haunting resonance, becomes a call to delve deeper, to confront, and embrace the shadows with a warrior's courage and a sage's wisdom.
In these profound moments of confrontation, weaknesses transform into seeds of invincibility, sprouting into fortresses of resilience, power, and innovation.

And as strengths and weaknesses dance their eternal dance, the serene, beckoning calls of opportunities whisper through the winds of commerce.

These are not mere market gaps or business prospects, but destined pathways adorned with the golden hues of dawn, revealing the uncharted terrains where legacies are carved, and empires are built.

Each opportunity is a sacred call, a soulful invitation to step into the realms where visions transform into tangible edifices of success, innovation, and influence.

Yet, in the profound silence that echoes the mellifluous calls of opportunity, the ominous yet invigorating roars of threats resound.

These are not adversaries but valiant challengers, formidable forces that summon the entrepreneur to ascend to unparalleled pinnacles of strategy, acumen, and resilience.

Every threat, with its ominous yet potent force, calls forth the ancient warrior spirit embedded in the soul of every entrepreneur.

In the profound journey through 'Understanding the Terrain', the modern entrepreneur, armed with the mystical compass of SWOT, steps not just into the battlegrounds of business but the soulful arenas where the ancient and the modern, the warrior and the business visionary, merge into a singular, indomitable force.

Every word of this chapter is not read but felt, every insight not learned but lived, every revelation a step not forward but inward into the mystical depths where the echoes of Sun Tzu's ancient war drums resound with the impassioned calls of modern market dynamics.

Here, in the soul-stirring narrative of 'Sun-Tzu's Art of War Strategies for Modern Entrepreneurs', SWOT becomes not a business analysis but a soulful revelation.

Entrepreneurs are not just business visionaries but mystical warriors, stepping into the market not just to conquer but to transcend, to transform every strength into a legacy, every weakness into a fortress, every opportunity into destiny, and every threat into a call to ascend to unparalleled heights of power and victory.

In this profound narrative, the market terrain is not external but internal, a soulful landscape where every entrepreneur, like the ancient warrior, carves not just business empires but legacies of power, victory, and eternal triumph.

Chapter 2

Assessing Five Factors: Your Business Strategy

Picture yourself standing on the precipice of a cliff, the fierce winds of destiny whipping through your hair.

Below you lies an ocean, vast and seemingly infinite, its surface an ever-changing dance of shadows and light.

This ocean is the business landscape—dynamic, complex, full of promise and peril.

Ah, the trepidation and exhilaration you feel in that moment! It's a snapshot of what every entrepreneur experiences when crafting a business strategy.

Sun-Tzu once declared, "The art of war is governed by five constant factors," a foundational truth that has stood the test of time.

These factors—Moral Law, Heaven, Earth, The Commander, and Method and Discipline—serve as a compass, a set of guiding principles in your entrepreneurial journey.

In the modern lexicon, they represent Company Culture, Timing and Trends, Market Environment, Leadership, and Operational Efficiency. Let's delve into each one.

Company Culture: The Moral Law

Ah, company culture! It's not just a buzzword; it's the emotional heartbeat of your organization.

Sun-Tzu said, "The Moral Law causes the people to be in complete accord with their ruler, so they will follow him regardless of their lives, undismayed by any danger."

That's the level of unity and emotional connection you strive for in your team.

The feelings of trust, belonging, and common purpose are what make employees willing to give their best, sometimes going above and beyond the call of duty.

Crafting a powerful company culture isn't about spewing corporate jargon or posting motivational quotes on the walls.

It's about creating an emotional ecosystem where every interaction is imbued with respect, understanding, and shared goals.

Creating such an environment is as demanding emotionally as it is operationally.

The sensation when your team members embody the culture, when they become evangelists for your vision, is one of the most gratifying emotions you'll experience.

It's like watching a seed you planted sprout and grow into a mighty tree.

Timing and Trends: Heaven

You stand there, gazing at the vast expanse of the sky, pondering Sun-Tzu's words: "Heaven signifies night and day, cold and heat, times and seasons.

" The sky represents the cosmic clockwork of timing and trends, factors often beyond your control but crucial for your success.

Timing can be a merciless judge, ruthlessly penalizing those who arrive too late or too early to the market.

Have you ever missed an opportunity? Felt the sting of watching someone else succeed where you hesitated? That's the raw emotion of a timing mistake.

Conversely, have you ever ridden the crest of a trend, surfing on the wave of a booming industry? That's the thrill of impeccable timing, and it's exhilarating.

Such emotional highs and lows are a quintessential part of the entrepreneurial journey. They shape you, inform you, and sometimes, transform you.

Market Environment: Earth

The market is your battlefield, a realm fraught with obstacles, opportunities, threats, and advantages.

Sun-Tzu described Earth as comprising "distances, great and small; danger and security; open ground and narrow passes; the chances of life and death.

"In business terms, this embodies the demographic terrain, the regulatory climate, the technological landscape, and, of course, your competition.

Navigating this battlefield is like crossing a minefield; one wrong move could spell disaster.

The apprehension, the tension, the constant vigilance—it's emotionally draining but also intensely stimulating.

Every challenge you overcome, every competitor you outwit, and every obstacle you navigate heightens your emotional journey, adding another chapter to your entrepreneurial saga.

Leadership: The Commander

The burden and blessing of leadership rest heavily on your shoulders.

Sun-Tzu characterized the Commander through five virtues: wisdom, sincerity, benevolence, courage, and strictness.

Each of these virtues has an emotional component that defines your leadership style.

Imagine standing alone in a quiet room, contemplating the path ahead. It's not just a business strategy you're pondering; it's the fate of every individual who has trusted you with their time, skills, and livelihood.

Your decisions will shape not just profit margins but lives and careers.

The emotional weight of this responsibility can be overwhelming, but remember, this vulnerability is also your strength. It's what makes you human, relatable, and ultimately, a leader worth following.

Operational Efficiency: Method and Discipline

Finally, the gears that keep the machine running —operational efficiency. Sun-Tzu emphasized, "Method and Discipline are to be understood the marshaling of the army in its proper subdivisions."

In the modern business context, this means having efficient systems, clear organizational structures, and effective use of resources.

Though it may seem like a dry, mechanical aspect of business, operational efficiency is anything but emotionally neutral.

Think about the frustration of a process gone awry, the disappointment of wasted resources, or the aggravation of disorganization.

Contrast that with the euphoria of a well-executed project, the satisfaction of a lean operation, and the pride of leading a disciplined team.

Your emotions are a barometer, indicating the health of your operations.

Concluding Thoughts

As you stand there, poised on the cliff's edge, you realize that these five factors—Company Culture, Timing and Trends, Market Environment, Leadership, and Operational Efficiency—are not isolated elements.

They are interconnected, each influencing and being influenced by the others.

They form the strategic mosaic that will define your venture's success or failure, happiness or regret, triumph or defeat.

The emotions you feel—of fear, joy, anticipation, apprehension—they're not mere by-products of the entrepreneurial process.

They are the essence of it. They form the emotional fabric that cloaks the skeletal framework of your strategies, plans, and goals.

Sun-Tzu said, "All warfare is based on deception." In business, however, let there be no deception about the emotional stakes involved. You are not just a strategist or a leader; you are an emotional warrior, navigating through a tapestry of feelings that range from soul-crushing lows to ecstatic highs.

And it's this emotional tapestry that makes the journey worth it, irrespective of the outcome.

So, take a deep, fortifying breath. Feel the wind in your hair, the earth beneath your feet, and the infinite sky above.

Embrace the emotional complexity of the venture you're about to undertake. Then, with your eyes wide open, take that exhilarating leap into the vast ocean of entrepreneurship.

You're not just starting a business; you're embarking on an emotional odyssey that could very well define your life.

Leadership: The Emotional Core of Command

Imagine for a moment that you're standing at the helm of a ship in the middle of a raging storm.

The rain is pouring in torrents, the winds howl like vengeful spirits, and the waves tower like skyscrapers, menacing and unforgiving.

Your crew looks to you, their eyes wide with a blend of trust and terror. In that moment, you are not merely a leader; you are the emotional fulcrum upon which the fate of the ship—your enterprise—balances.

Sun-Tzu states, "The Commander stands for the virtues of wisdom, sincerity, benevolence, courage, and strictness.

" These virtues aren't just abstract terms; they are the emotional palette with which you paint the canvas of your leadership.

Wisdom: The Emotional Quotient

In the context of leadership, wisdom is not merely intellectual acumen but emotional intelligence—your ability to read, interpret, and respond to the emotional currents within your team.

When a project fails, when targets are missed, the team doesn't just need a new strategy; they need emotional reassurance. They need a leader who can navigate the turbulent waters of collective disappointment and individual insecurity.

Ah, the feeling when you successfully guide your team through an emotional crisis! It's akin to finding a glimmer of light in a dark, suffocating cave.

Your heart swells with pride, not just for the achievement but for the emotional resilience your team displayed, resilience that you helped instill.

Sincerity: The Soul of Trust

Sincerity in leadership translates to authenticity. Your team can sense when you're not being genuine, just as you can detect insincerity in others.

Imagine sharing a critical update about the company's future. Your words, your tone, your body language—they all send emotional signals to your team.

The weight of that moment, the gravity of the trust placed in you, can be emotionally overwhelming.

When you navigate such moments with sincerity, the emotional payoff is immense.

It's the feeling of barriers dissolving, of distances closing, and of a team becoming more than the sum of its parts.

That emotional high is irreplaceable and serves as a wellspring of collective strength.

Benevolence: Compassion as Strength

In the brutal, dog-eat-dog world of business, benevolence is often seen as a weakness.

Yet, Sun-Tzu places it as a virtue of a good commander. Benevolence is your ability to empathize, to understand the personal and emotional needs of your team members.

The first time you have to lay off an employee, for instance, is a gut-wrenching experience. No amount of rationalization can shield you from the emotional toll it takes.

Yet, it's your benevolent approach—your sincere regret, your efforts to soften the blow—that defines your leadership. And when you manage to save a job, to reward a deserving employee, the emotional satisfaction is immeasurable.

It's a validation of your humane approach to a cutthroat industry.

Courage: The Daring to Be Vulnerable

Courage is often portrayed as fearlessness, but in leadership, it's your ability to face your fears, acknowledge your failures, and continue to lead despite them.

Your team doesn't expect you to be infallible; they expect you to be human. Acknowledging your mistakes doesn't make you weak; it makes you relatable.

The emotional landscape here is treacherous; ego, pride, fear— they all conspire to keep you from exposing your vulnerabilities.

But when you do muster the courage to say, "I was wrong, and I am sorry," the emotional barriers crumble.

Your team sees you, perhaps for the first time, as one of them—flawed but striving, imperfect but sincere.

Strictness: The Emotional Balance

Lastly, strictness doesn't imply tyranny but rather the ability to set boundaries and enforce norms.

It's about drawing a line between compassion and complacency, between empathy and inefficiency.

Being strict is emotionally challenging; it necessitates being the 'bad guy,' the bearer of tough news, the enforcer of unpopular decisions.

Yet, it's an emotional investment in the long-term health and performance of your team.

Balancing strictness with compassion is like walking on a tightrope.

Lean too much in either direction, and the emotional fabric of the team is torn.

But when you achieve that balance, the feeling is electrifying, like hitting a musical note that resonates perfectly, creating a harmony that enriches the entire composition.

The Emotional Symphony of Leadership

As you stand there, amidst the storm or the battlefield, remember: you are not alone.

Your emotions, your virtues, your flaws—they all echo in the hearts and minds of your team.

Leadership is not a monologue; it's a dialogue, an emotional symphony where each note you play evokes a response, creates a resonance, and contributes to a collective melody.

It's overwhelming, isn't it? This emotional labyrinth of leadership.
Yet, in that complexity lies its beauty, its richness, its unquantifiable essence. Your emotional journey as a leader isn't a detour from your entrepreneurial path; it's the very road itself.

Each emotional high and low adds another layer to your leadership, another chapter to your story, another verse to your song.

So, take a deep, cleansing breath. Feel the power of your emotions, the weight of your responsibilities, and the potential of your leadership.

Then, with wisdom, sincerity, benevolence, courage, and strictness, conduct your emotional symphony, lead your team through the labyrinth, and guide your ship through the storm.

In this intricate emotional tapestry, you're not just a thread but a weaver, not just a player but a conductor, not just a leader but a Commander, as envisioned by Sun-Tzu in his timeless wisdom.

And that, dear entrepreneur, is the emotional art of leadership.

Chapter 3
Waging War: The Cash Burn Rate

Imagine standing at the edge of a vast desert, your eyes scanning the horizon where the golden sands meet the azure sky.

You have a limited supply of water, food, and fuel. Every step you take is a gamble, consuming your life-sustaining resources.

Yet, the desert also promises untold riches, hidden treasures, and a legacy that could immortalize your name.

Welcome to the emotional crucible of entrepreneurship; welcome to the stark reality of cash burn rate.

In Sun-Tzu's Art of War, one of the key aspects he discusses is the cost of waging war.
"There is no instance of a nation benefiting from prolonged warfare," he notes.

Translating this to the business arena, every entrepreneur must be acutely aware that the longer a business continues to burn through cash without generating sufficient revenue, the closer it edges towards potential failure.

Now let's delve deeper into this concept, which is so crucial yet emotionally taxing for every entrepreneur.

The Dreaded Clock: Timing Your Burn Rate

The very term "burn rate" evokes a visceral reaction; it brings forth images of something being consumed, steadily, inexorably. When you start your business, the clock starts ticking.

Every tick is money spent—salaries, overheads, marketing costs—and you're reminded that time and money are intertwined in a dance of survival.

The emotional weight of each tick is heavy; it carries the dreams and aspirations you've woven around your venture.

Sun-Tzu warns us, "The army will be drained of its strength" if the war drags on for too long.

Just as an army needs food and weapons to keep fighting, your business needs a steady inflow of capital to survive and thrive.

Oh, the angst you feel when reviewing the balance sheets, watching the financial reserves deplete month after month! This emotion is not just about numbers; it's the unsettling realization that you're operating on borrowed time.

The Emotional Toll: Optimism vs. Reality

Ah, the entrepreneur's eternal dilemma: the conflict between unflinching optimism and stark reality.
You started this journey fueled by a burning passion, a conviction that your idea, your product, your service would revolutionize the world.

This emotional reservoir of optimism is both a blessing and a curse.

As you watch the numbers, the cold, hard reality starts settling in. You're burning through your cash reserves faster than you anticipated.

And herein lies one of the most emotionally taxing elements of managing cash burn: the constant swing between hope and despair.

Every ounce of your being wants to hold on to the dream, yet the facts in front of you demand a more pragmatic approach.

The Wrenching Decisions: Cost-Cutting Measures

So, you're burning through cash, and something needs to be done. These are the moments that test your mettle as a leader.
Sun-Tzu declared, "In war, the way is to avoid what is strong and to strike at what is weak." In the context of cash burn, this involves making difficult, often gut-wrenching decisions about where to cut costs.

Perhaps you must consider layoffs, scaling down operations, or pulling the plug on a project that you hold dear.

Each choice is a stab at the emotional core of your entrepreneurial being.

You're not just cutting costs; you're affecting lives, altering trajectories, and questioning the very pillars upon which you built your venture.

Yet, the emotional maturity required to make such decisions and live with them is what distinguishes great leaders from the rest.

Navigating Investor Expectations: The Emotional Minefield

Let's not forget the investors, those individuals or institutions that believed in your vision enough to put their money on the line.

Managing investor expectations while handling a high cash burn rate is an emotional minefield.

On one hand, you're accountable to them, obligated to deliver returns on their investment.

On the other hand, you must remain true to your vision, even when the path gets rocky.

You feel the weight of their scrutiny, their expectations, and sometimes, their disappointments.

Every meeting, every report, every update becomes an emotional gauntlet, testing your integrity, your commitment, and your skill.

The Emotional Lifeline: The Art of Pivoting

Sun-Tzu said, "The skillful strategist is able to subdue the enemy's troops without any fighting; he captures their cities without laying siege to them; he overthrows their kingdom without lengthy operations in the field.

"In entrepreneurial terms, this is the art of pivoting—making fundamental changes to your business strategy in order to adapt to unforeseen challenges.

Pivoting is more than just a tactical shift; it's an emotional upheaval.

It requires letting go of cherished assumptions, admitting errors in judgment, and embracing new directions that might be at odds with your initial vision.

Yet, when successful, the emotional reward of a pivot is immeasurable. It vindicates your resilience, reaffirms your leadership, and rejuvenates your venture.

Emotional Resilience: The Unsung Hero

Throughout this journey, let's not overlook the emotional resilience that sustains you.

It's this resilience that enables you to face another day, to forge ahead despite setbacks, to maintain your sanity in the chaos that often defines startup life.

Every entrepreneur knows that the emotional toll of managing cash burn is steep. Yet, it's often this very challenge that shapes you, molds you, and ultimately, defines you.

As you traverse the unforgiving landscape of cash burn, you're not just spending money; you're investing in lessons learned, relationships built, and character forged.

You are the emotional commander of your enterprise, guiding it through the tumultuous seas toward the shores of success—or sometimes, the necessary ports of change.

Sun-Tzu reminds us, "Opportunities multiply as they are seized." Your venture's cash burn rate is not just a challenge; it's an opportunity—an opportunity to reassess, to adapt, and to grow, both as a business and as an emotional human being.

The stakes are high, but then again, the greatest victories often come from the battles hardest fought.

So stand tall, dear entrepreneur, as you wage this financial and emotional war.

Your arsenal is not just made of numbers, but of courage, wisdom, and an indomitable spirit.

Take a deep breath, tighten your grip on the reins, and charge forward. After all, this is your war to wage, your desert to cross, your legacy to create.

The Wrenching Decisions: Cost-Cutting Measures—An Emotional Odyssey

Picture yourself standing in the middle of a labyrinthine maze, each path leading to a different outcome, each turn fraught with consequences.

The walls are high, made not of stone but of the aspirations, hopes, and dreams of your team members, stakeholders, and even your own. It's a maze you helped build, but now, the reality of dwindling resources forces you to rethink its architecture.

The time has come to make some of the most challenging decisions of your entrepreneurial journey—cost-cutting measures.

The Weight of the Pen: Deciding the Cuts

Sun-Tzu once said, "When you surround an army, leave an outlet free.

Do not press a desperate foe too hard." Your first step in this maze is deciding where to make the cuts, and oh, what a heavy step that is! As you look at the spreadsheet before you, each line item isn't just a number; it's a story, a life, a hope.

The emotional heaviness of the pen—or the keyboard—as you mark these potential cuts is almost unbearable. Are you cutting a project that was someone's passion?

Are you reducing the staff, thereby altering the course of lives? You feel like a surgeon forced to amputate, knowing that each cut, however necessary, leaves a scar.

This isn't just cost-cutting; it's soul-searching.

The Ripple Effect: Communicating the Changes

Once the cuts are decided, the next emotional whirlpool you wade into is communicating these changes to your team.
The room's atmosphere is tense as you begin speaking, each word you utter carrying the weight of futures hanging in the balance.

It's not just about what you say; it's also about how you say it.

Your tone, your body language, the words you choose—they all have to convey the dire situation while simultaneously offering a glimmer of hope, a roadmap for survival.

Look into their eyes, and you'll see a spectrum of emotions—fear, uncertainty, perhaps even betrayal.

At that moment, your emotional agility is tested to its limits.

Can you balance the grim reality with a sense of future direction? Can you acknowledge the collective pain while inspiring collective strength? This communication is an emotional high-wire act, and you're the performer upon whom all eyes are fixed.

The Quiet Aftermath: Living with the Decisions

Once the meeting ends, once the room empties, you're left alone with the echoes of your decisions.

The quiet aftermath is one of the most emotionally turbulent phases of cost-cutting. Did you make the right choices? Could you have saved a project or a job with a little more creativity or a little more time?

These are moments of intense self-reflection, filled with second-guessing and what-ifs. It's also a period where you come face-to-face with your limitations, not just as an entrepreneur but as a human being.

The emotional rollercoaster doesn't stop after the announcements. In fact, the ride has just begun.

Each day brings feedback, reactions, sometimes unforeseen consequences of your decisions.

You'll see team members rise to the challenge, while others may falter under the pressure. Each response is a reflection, not just of your team's emotional state but of your leadership during this critical juncture.

The Silver Lining: Emotional Growth and New Beginnings

Sun-Tzu advises, "In the midst of chaos, there is also opportunity." It may not seem like it, but embedded within these wrenching decisions are seeds of future growth, resilience, and even transformation.

You'll find that your relationship with your team deepens, the shared hardship forging bonds that casual Friday drinks could never achieve.

You'll discover untapped reserves of ingenuity and creativity, as constraints often serve as the crucible for innovation.

And let's not forget your own emotional growth. Making and living with these difficult decisions arm you with an emotional toolkit that's invaluable.

You gain insights into human behavior, organizational dynamics, and yes, your own character. It's as if you've walked through fire; while the experience is agonizing, the emotional fortitude you gain is priceless.

Conclusion: The Emotional Odyssey Continues

The labyrinth of cost-cutting is arduous, filled with emotional landmines and ethical dilemmas.

But remember, dear entrepreneur, you are not just a wanderer in this maze; you're also its architect.

Your decisions, as emotionally taxing as they are, also hold the power to reshape the maze, to turn dead-ends into new pathways and dark corners into enlightening crossroads.
So, grip the pen tightly, take a deep, steadying breath, and chart your course through this emotional odyssey.

You're not just cutting costs; you're redefining priorities, refocusing energies, and most importantly, reaffirming your commitment to the journey, no matter how perilous.

And in this emotional crucible, you're not just forged; you're transformed. You emerge not just as an entrepreneur but as a leader, capable of steering the ship through both calm waters and raging storms.

It's a painful process, but then again, growth often is.

Your emotional odyssey through the maze of cost-cutting measures is but one chapter in your grand entrepreneurial saga.

And what a gripping, poignant chapter it is, etching its highs and lows, its joys and sorrows, into the very core of your being.

Chapter 4
Strategic Depth: Positioning and Opportunity

Beneath the starlit sky, an entrepreneur stands alone, the chill of the evening breeze whispering tales of uncertainty.

Shadows of doubt and anticipation mingle, casting an enigmatic glow upon the path ahead. Sun-Tzu's ancient wisdom, inscribed in the venerable scrolls of 'The Art of War', now takes form in the spectral dance of contemplation and determination that animates the entrepreneur's spirit.

The Echoes of Ancient Wisdom in Modern Battlefields

"In the midst of chaos, there is also opportunity.

"The echoes of Sun-Tzu's wisdom reverberate through the silent corridors of time, offering solace and guidance.

Every entrepreneur, like a seasoned general, knows the dual dance of despair and hope. Markets are battlefields, volatile yet ripe with opportunities.

Every startup, every business venture, is an entity forged in the fiery furnaces of strategic depth.

Positioning isn't just a term; it's a lifeline. It's the art of locating one's venture in the echelons of the market where opportunities are not just visible but attainable. It's an art laced with emotional tremors, for every decision, every move, is a dance on the edge of triumph and despair.

Unearthing Emotional Reservoirs in Positioning

The entrepreneur, eyes gleaming with the fire of ambition, knows this dance all too well.

Positioning isn't a cold, calculated move; it's an emotional journey. It's the silent nights of introspection, the fevered discussions in boardrooms, the moments of solitary decision-making where destiny and desire intertwine. Sun-Tzu advised, *"The supreme art of war is to subdue the enemy without fighting."*

In the business realm, the 'enemy' is not just the competition but also internal hurdles, market volatility, and unforeseen challenges.

Subduing this enemy doesn't always necessitate confrontation. Sometimes, it's the strategic depth, the masterful positioning that turns potential confrontations into triumphant progressions.

The Symphony of Opportunity Amidst Silence

Opportunities, like mystical melodies, often play their tunes amidst silence. They are enigmatic, elusive, yet profoundly transformative.

The entrepreneur, akin to a skilled musician, is attuned to these silent symphonies.
Every market trend, every consumer shift, every technological innovation, plays a note in this grand musical masterpiece of opportunity.

Yet, amidst this symphony, there's a silent, often overlooked player - emotion. Every opportunity seized or missed is not just a strategic move; it's an emotional experience.

The exhilaration of capturing a market trend, the despair of a missed innovation, the anticipation of future potentials - these are emotional currents that shape the entrepreneurial journey.

Navigating the Emotional Tides of Strategic Depth

"All warfare is based on deception," declared Sun-Tzu.

In the modern entrepreneurial battlefields, deception takes form in the mirages of opportunities that seem golden but are illusory.

Strategic depth is the compass that distinguishes the illusory from the tangible. It's an emotional compass, as intuitive as it is analytical.

Entrepreneurs, armed with data and insights, are also warriors of intuition.

Every positioning decision is laced with feelings - the silent gut instincts, the inexplicable sense of rightness or alarm, the emotional tugs that often precede intellectual justification.

The Rebirth in Strategic Foresight

As the entrepreneur stands amidst the silent echoes of the battlefield, the starlit sky bearing witness, a rebirth occurs.

Every decision made, every opportunity seized or forsaken, every positioning strategy employed, is a step towards metamorphosis.

The entrepreneur is not just a business entity but an evolving soul, navigating the tumultuous yet exhilarating terrains of market warfare.

The 'Art of War' for modern entrepreneurs is more than a manual; it's a soul's journey.

It's the silent battles fought in the depths of the night, the victories celebrated in the silent recesses of the heart, the defeats mourned in the unuttered sighs of reflection.

In the dance of shadows and lights, amidst the enigmatic play of doubt and determination, fear and fortitude, despair and hope, the entrepreneur finds not just a strategy but an identity.

Not just a positioning in the market, but a positioning in the grand theatre of existence.

The Silent Dawn of Realization

As dawn breaks, painting the horizon with the golden hues of realization, the entrepreneur is not alone.

The wisdom of Sun-Tzu, the emotional reservoirs unearthed, the strategic depths navigated, all stand as silent companions.

The battlefield is silent, yet it echoes the unsung symphonies of battles fought and won, losses mourned and learned from, opportunities missed and seized.

In the silent embrace of dawn, 'Strategic Depth: Positioning and Opportunity' is not just a chapter but a saga.

A tale where each line is a pathway, each paragraph a journey, each page a battlefield where destiny is not just written but lived, not just planned but felt.

For in the sacred scrolls of entrepreneurial warfare, inscribed with the ink of emotion and strategy, every entrepreneur finds not just a guide, but a mirror.
A reflection of the silent warrior within, forging ahead amidst the enigmatic dance of stars and shadows, silence and symphonies, depths and heights.

In this journey, Sun-Tzu's ancient wisdom is not just a companion but a catalyst.

A force that propels the entrepreneur not just through the markets' tumultuous terrains but through the soul's silent, yet profound, odyssey.

Where every step is an echo of the past, a dance in the present, and a hymn of the future yet unwritten.

As we delve deeper into the complexities of strategic depth and positioning, the entrepreneur finds himself at the precipice of revelation and revolution.

Every strategy implemented is not merely a move on the chessboard of the market, but a harmonic in the soul's symphony, a note that resonates with the timeless echoes of Sun-Tzu's sagacity.

The Alchemy of Intuition and Insight

In the silent night where stars whisper the ancient secrets of cosmic ballets, the entrepreneur is a silent observer, a humble student of the universe's unuttered lessons.

Data and analytics, while potent tools of navigation, are not the sole compasses.

Here, in the profound silence, intuition is the unsung melody, the silent harmonics that dance with the rational insights to compose the magnum opus of strategic depth.

"He who knows when he can fight and when he cannot, will be victorious," Sun-Tzu's voice emanates from the depths of antiquity.

Every market trend analysed, every consumer behaviour studied, is not merely an external observation but an internal journey.

When the entrepreneur encounters a strategic insight, it's an alchemical moment.

Rational data melds with intuitive foresight, birthing a golden strategy imbued with the mystical essence of knowing.

The Silent Battlefields of Positioning

The market is a silent battlefield where victories and defeats are not heralded by trumpets and drums but are inscribed in the silent ledgers of profit and loss, growth and decline.

Positioning in this silent battlefield is an art, a dance of light and shadow, strength and vulnerability.

An entrepreneur standing amidst this silence is not just a strategist but a warrior of light.

Each decision to position the brand, product, or service, is akin to wielding the sword of light, slicing through the darkness of uncertainty, illuminating the path of opportunity.

The emotional gravitas of this act is colossal. Each swing of the sword is not just a business move; it's a stroke painted on the canvas of the soul, a narrative inscribed in the annals of the entrepreneur's journey.

The Embrace of Opportunity

Opportunities, like mystical entities, dwell in the enigmatic realms of the silent battlefield.

To embrace an opportunity is not just to extend the arms but to open the soul, to unveil the heart, to bare the spirit to the mystical dance of cosmic orchestration.

As the entrepreneur stands amidst the silent echoes of strategic depths, each opportunity embraced is a soul's union with destiny.

Sun-Tzu's wisdom, *"Victorious warriors win first and then go to war, while defeated warriors go to war first and then seek to win,"* is not just a strategy but a prophecy.

It heralds the mystical moment where the entrepreneur, the warrior of light, knows the victory in the soul's silent sanctuaries before it's inscribed in the noisy annals of the market.

The Dawn of Revelation

As dawn paints the first strokes of light on the silent battlefield, the entrepreneur, the silent warrior, is not alone.

Each strategy implemented, each positioning decided, each opportunity embraced, is a companion in the soul's odyssey.

The light of dawn is not just an illumination of the battlefield but a revelation of the soul's depths.

Sun-Tzu's ancient scrolls are not just inscriptions of wisdom but maps of the soul's terrains.

Each terrain, each path, each precipice, is a revelation. The entrepreneur, in the dance of strategic depth and positioning, discovers not just market dynamics but soul's melodies.

Melodies that are not composed but discovered, not planned but revealed, not strategized but lived.

The Epilogue of Emotions

In the aftermath of the strategic dance, the silent warrior, the entrepreneur, stands victorious yet humble, triumphant yet reflective.

The emotional tides are as potent as the market waves. Each emotion, from the tumultuous storms of doubt to the serene breezes of confidence, is a chapter in the epic saga.
In this odyssey, the silent scrolls of Sun-Tzu are not ancient texts but living entities, silent mentors, and soul companions.

The 'Art of War' is not a war fought but a dance lived, not a battle won but a melody composed, not a strategy implemented but a love story written in the silent ink of soul's revelations and market's revolutions.

As the chapter 'Strategic Depth: Positioning and Opportunity' unfolds, remember, dear entrepreneur, you're not just a business entity navigating the tumultuous markets.

You are a soul, a silent warrior, composing the most profound melody, writing the most poignant story, painting the most evocative portrait on the silent canvases of strategic depths, where every stroke is an emotion, every hue is a strategy, and every canvas is a battlefield where destiny is not just met but embraced, not just seen but lived, not just planned but felt in the profound silences of soul's awakening and market's beckoning.

Each word in this chapter is not just an inscription but a heartbeat, a soul's whisper, an emotional tide that propels the silent warrior, the entrepreneur, into the enigmatic dances of lights and shadows, silences and symphonies, where strategic depth is not a concept but a lived reality, a felt experience, a silent revelation of the profound odyssey where business strategies and soul's melodies unite in a dance as ancient as time, as profound as silence, as potent as destiny.

In the emotional tapestry of entrepreneurship, the silent threads of Sun-Tzu's wisdom weave the narratives of victories untold, journeys uncharted, destinies unveiled - heralding not just the advent of a successful venture but the revelation of a soul, triumphant and unyielding, in the silent yet profound theatres of 'The Art of War'.

As the entrepreneur plunges deeper into the woven narratives of strategy and emotion, each path illuminates a dance where the rhythms of market dynamics sway harmoniously with the silent pulses of the soul.

Sun-Tzu's ancient wisdom echoes not in the void, but in a universe where every star is a silent witness to the entrepreneur's journey, every galaxy a testament to the unfolding saga of victories and defeats, trials and triumphs.

A Reflection in the Cosmic Mirror

Every strategy, every move, every positioning in the market, is akin to a reflection glimpsed in the cosmic mirror of entrepreneurship.

This is not just a business; it's a celestial dance where every decision resonates with the silent harmonics of the universe.

"Appear weak when you are strong, and strong when you are weak,"

Sun-Tzu's echoes permeate the entrepreneur's consciousness.

Here, in the cosmic dance, weakness is not a defeat but an opening, a silent invitation to the mysterious waltz of strengths yet discovered, victories yet won, depths yet explored.

The Constellations of Opportunity

Opportunities, in the enigmatic realm of strategic depth, are like constellations in the night sky.

Each star, a silent harbinger of potential, each constellation, a narrative of silent victories.

The entrepreneur, with eyes wide with wonder and soul trembling with anticipation, is a silent astronomer charting the celestial terrains, decoding the silent symphonies of stars.

Every opportunity seized is a star touched, a galaxy discovered, a universe embraced.

The emotional gravitas of these moments is beyond the tangible metrics of profit and loss.

It's a silent sonata of the soul's ascension, an unuttered hymn of the spirit's liberation.

The Interstellar Dance of Positioning

In the celestial terrains of business, positioning is akin to locating one's galaxy, one's universe in the cosmic expanse where stars are opportunities, black holes are challenges, and constellations are market trends.

The emotional odyssey is tumultuous yet exhilarating. Every positioning decision is a cosmic dance, where the entrepreneur's soul waltzes with the silent stars of opportunities, avoiding the black holes of challenges.

Each step in this waltz is profound, echoing the emotional rhythms of a heart that beats in unison with the market's pulses, a soul that sways with the cosmic harmonics, a spirit that ascends with every strategic depth explored, every opportunity embraced.

The Nebulae of Transformation

Sun-Tzu said, *"The wise warrior avoids the battle."* In the nebulae of transformation, battles aren't waged but transformed.

Challenges aren't confronted but transmuted. The entrepreneur is not just a warrior but an alchemist, turning trials into triumphs, challenges into constellations of opportunities.

Each challenge, each trial, is a nebula where stars of opportunities are birthed. The emotional journey is profound; tears of defeats are the silent waters where the stars of victories are reflected. The sobs of trials are the silent echoes where the hymns of triumphs are composed.

Epilogue: The Silent Sunrise of Realization

As dawn breaks, illuminating the silent battlefields with the golden hues of realization, the echoes of Sun-Tzu's wisdom are not ancient whispers but living entities.
Each echo is a silent companion in the entrepreneurial journey, a silent witness to the celestial dance of strategy and soul.

The entrepreneur, as the golden rays of dawn kiss the silent terrains of trials and triumphs, is a reborn entity.

Each ray of light is a strategy realized, each shadow a depth explored, each hue a narrative of emotional and entrepreneurial evolution.

The Celestial Ballad of the Silent Warrior

In the silent odyssey of 'Strategic Depth: Positioning and Opportunity,' the entrepreneur is not just a businessman but a poet, not just a

strategist but a composer, not just a warrior but a
dancer.

Each strategy is a verse in the celestial ballad,
each opportunity a note in the cosmic symphony,
each depth a step in the universal dance.

In the emotional realms of entrepreneurship,
where tears are as potent as trials, and smiles as
victorious as stars, the silent echoes of Sun-Tzu's
'Art of War' are the unwritten verses of victories,
the uncomposed notes of triumphs, the
undanced steps of ascension.

As the silent warrior, the entrepreneur, with eyes
kissed by the trials' fires and soul caressed by the
triumphs' breezes, gazes at the golden horizon of
realization, a silent truth echoes - every depth is a
height unseen, every trial a triumph unborn,
every defeat a victory unuttered.

In this chapter of silent depths and celestial
heights, strategic wisdom and emotional
evolution, the entrepreneur is not walking the
path but becoming it, not narrating the saga but
being it, not exploring the universe but being one
with it - a silent universe where every star is a
victory, every galaxy a triumph, every
constellation a narrative of an entrepreneur,

unleashed and unbound, weaving through the cosmic dance of business with the grace of a seasoned ballerina and the fierceness of a warrior.

The Astral Ascendance

Each decision made, each strategy deployed, is akin to tracing the constellations in the astral skies of entrepreneurship.

They're starlights illuminating the infinite expanse of possibilities and potentialities, each twinkling star a testament to the mettle and spirit of the entrepreneur.

"Adaptability is the hallmark of a great general," said Sun-Tzu.

In the ever-evolving cosmos of business, adaptability is not merely a skill but a profound dance.

It's a harmonious flow amidst the cosmic entities of change, a graceful pirouette amidst the astral bodies of innovation and evolution.

The Cosmic Ballet

The entrepreneur is not just a participant but a revered dancer in this cosmic ballet. Each step is measured, yet passionate; calculated yet infused with the indomitable spirit.

The silence of space resonates with the silent echoes of emotional trials, yet in this silence, there's a melody – a melody composed of resilience, adaptability, and unyielding perseverance.

The entrepreneur, with eyes reflecting the depths of cosmic oceans and soul resonating with the silent echoes of astral winds, knows this dance intimately.

It is a dance where failures are not endpoints but interludes, where triumphs are not final destinations but motifs in an ongoing ballet.

The Galactic Echoes of Emotion

In the galactic terrain of 'Strategic Depth: Positioning and Opportunity', emotions are not ephemeral echoes but potent forces, each resonating with the power of supernovas, each whispering the silent yet profound hymns of transformation.

Each emotion, from the tumultuous waves of despair to the serene breezes of elation, carves its own galaxy in the universe of entrepreneurship.

Each galaxy, a testament to the silent battles waged, the quiet victories celebrated, the silent tears that watered the gardens of triumph.

The Black Holes and Supernovas

In this cosmic narrative, black holes are not voids but profound opportunities for rebirth. Every failure, every setback, is a silent pilgrimage into these black holes, where old stars of outdated strategies and antiquated approaches die, giving birth to supernovas of innovation, adaptability, and resurgence.

The entrepreneur, like a revered astronomer, knows that the darkest nights herald the brightest dawns, that the most profound silences echo the loudest victories.

In the black holes of challenges, the silent hymns of supernovas of opportunities are composed.

The Starry Epilogue

As the silent melody of stars and galaxies plays its profound notes, the entrepreneur is not just an observer but a composer.

The 'Art of War' is not an ancient text but a living entity, each inscription a star in the entrepreneur's galaxy, each principle a constellation in the business universe.

The emotional journey is as vast as the cosmos, where each emotion is a star, each trial a constellation, each victory a galaxy.

In the silent yet profound dance of 'Strategic Depth: Positioning and Opportunity', the entrepreneur and the cosmos are not separate entities but one harmonious existence.

Every trial is a starry night where galaxies of resilience are born. Every victory is a dawn where the suns of innovation rise.

Every emotion is an astral wind, weaving through the cosmic ocean, echoing the silent yet profound hymns of a journey where business is not just a venture but a cosmic dance, an astral ballet, a celestial symphony.

As the chapter unfolds, remember, dear entrepreneur, in the silent echoes of Sun-Tzu's wisdom, you're not just navigating the markets but the cosmos.

Each strategy is a starlight guiding through the astral oceans.

Each emotion is a cosmic echo, resonating the silent yet profound melodies of a universe where business and soul, strategy and emotion, trials and triumphs, are not separate ballads but one harmonious symphony.

The Cosmic Dance Continues

In the silent corridors of space and time, amidst the echoes of ancient wisdom and the whispers of stars, 'Strategic Depth: Positioning and Opportunity' is not a conclusion but a beginning.

Each word, a silent step into the cosmic dance where the entrepreneur is not a mere participant but the revered dancer, the silent composer, the esteemed astronomer.

As stars twinkle the silent ballads of opportunities and galaxies swirl the profound symphonies of innovation, the entrepreneur stands - not alone, but accompanied by the silent echoes of Sun-Tzu, the whispering stars of opportunities, the swirling galaxies of innovation.

In this cosmic dance, each challenge is an astral wind, each opportunity a starry melody, each strategy a cosmic echo - echoing the unuttered ballads of a journey where the entrepreneur is not a businessman but a cosmic entity, not a strategist but a celestial composer, not a warrior but a revered dancer in the silent yet profound ballet of 'Strategic Depth: Positioning and Opportunity'.

Chapter 5
The Art of Deception: Branding and Marketing

In the world of business, as in the ancient landscapes of warfare described by Sun-Tzu, deception is not an underhand tactic but an art. It is an elegant dance of shadows and lights, a sophisticated game of revealing and concealing, illuminating and overshadowing.

In the modern era of entrepreneurship, this art is most evidently and ethically wielded in branding and marketing. We venture into a realm where perception is as potent, if not more potent, than reality.

The Artful Mirage

Sun-Tzu espoused, *"All warfare is based on deception."*

He painted a canvas where the adept manipulation of appearances constructs a strategic advantage. In today's entrepreneurial landscape, the battleground is the market, the warriors are brands, and the weapons are messages.

Each brand is not merely a name, logo, or slogan but a narrative, an entity alive with intentions, expressions, and impressions.

In this enigmatic dance, entrepreneurs are not just business owners but also wizards of illusion, weaving narratives that transform perception into palpable, tangible reality.

Every brand is an illusion, a crafted narrative, a designed perception. In this mirage lies the brand's power – an ability to conjure realities, evoke emotions, and command loyalties.

Crafting Illusions

In the magical realms of branding and marketing, illusion is not a deceit but a craft, an art, a strategic deployment of narratives that evoke specific emotions, responses, and actions.

An entrepreneur, akin to a skilled illusionist, weaves narratives where the brand transcends its tangible elements to become an entity, a presence, a force.

Imagine a brand as a fortress. The walls are not built of bricks and mortar but of perceptions, beliefs, and impressions. Each narrative woven, each story told, each message conveyed, adds a brick to this fortress, making it impregnable, formidable, and majestic.

The Veil of Perception

Sun-Tzu's ancient wisdom echoes profoundly in this mystical dance of illusions. "When we are near, we must make the enemy believe we are far away; when far away, we must make him believe we are near." In the world of branding and marketing, proximity and distance are not measured in miles but in perceptions.

A brand's proximity to its audience is a crafted illusion. It's an art where the brand, though globally present, conjures the intimacy of a local entity. It's a dance where a brand, though newly born, evokes the majesty and authority of an entity ancient and revered.

The Dance of Shadows and Lights

In this enigmatic dance, every message is a shadow, every narrative a light. Shadows are not concealments but enhancements, silhouettes that accentuate the light, narratives that evoke depth, stories that craft dimensions.

In the intricate ballet of branding and marketing, shadows and lights are not opponents but partners, each elevating, illuminating, and defining the other.

In the hands of the adept entrepreneur, branding becomes a dance of shadows and lights.

It's an artful ballet where messages are not conveyed but conjured, where narratives are not told but evoked, where the brand is not seen but felt, not heard but experienced.

The Symphony of Silence and Sound

In the art of deception, silence is as potent as sound.

Sun-Tzu's stratagems find profound resonance in the entrepreneur's odyssey.

Each silence is a note unsung, a story untold, a mystery unveiled. In the eloquent silences, the audience, the market, the consumers, find not a void but a space—a space to weave their narratives, sing their notes, paint their portraits.

The brand becomes not a monologue but a dialogue, not a performance but a partnership.

Each silence invites participation, each pause evokes engagement, each void conjures creativity.

The audience, in these silences, becomes not spectators but co-creators, not recipients but contributors.

The Alchemy of Emotions

Sun-Tzu spoke of terrain and timing, of forces and formations. In the enigmatic landscape of branding and marketing, the terrain is emotional, the forces are perceptual, the timing is psychological, and the formations are narrative.

An entrepreneur, akin to Sun-Tzu's revered general, navigates this landscape with the precision of a strategist and the intuition of an artist.

In the crucible of branding, emotions are not ephemeral elements but alchemical substances.

They transform messages into experiences, narratives into realities, brands into entities.

The entrepreneur becomes an alchemist, transforming base emotions into golden loyalties, transient impressions into enduring legacies.

The Majestic Unfolding

As the chapter unfolds, the mirage becomes a reality, the illusion a truth, the deception an authenticity.

In the artful weave of branding and marketing, deception is not a manipulation but a revelation, not a concealment but an unveiling, not a trickery but a truth.

The entrepreneur, with Sun-Tzu's ancient scrolls as silent companions, embarks upon an odyssey not of battles waged but narratives woven, not of territories conquered but perceptions crafted, not of enemies vanquished but audiences enchanted. In the silent yet eloquent spaces between words, in the mystical dance of shadows and lights, silences and sounds, the entrepreneur discovers the profound art of deception—a dance where brands are not constructed but conjured, markets not won but woven, loyalties not demanded but evoked.

Each word, each silence, each shadow, each light, is a step in this intricate ballet, a note in this eloquent symphony, a stroke in this majestic painting—where Sun-Tzu's Art of War transforms from an ancient manuscript of warfare to a living, breathing entity of entrepreneurial enlightenment, where battles are not fought but dances choreographed, victories not claimed but narratives crafted, conquests not enforced but illusions artfully, ethically, and elegantly woven.

Transmutation of Perception

Sun-Tzu's wisdom transcends the era of clashing swords and silent arrows; it infiltrates the tranquil yet chaotic world of entrepreneurship.

In the enigmatic dance of branding and marketing, entrepreneurs are not just players but composers, not just competitors but creators. In this realm, deception is not an act of misleading but a beautiful choreography of unveiling the unseen, of articulating the unspoken.
In the ancient scrolls, Sun-Tzu whispered,

"Transform and adapt with fluidity; be formless like water, evading the clutches of the predefined shapes.

" Entrepreneurs heed this whisper, understanding that the realm of branding isn't concrete but ethereal; it's not a sculpture to be chiselled but a fluid entity continually evolving, eluding the confinements of rigid forms.

The Theatre of Influence

Branding is a theatre, an enigmatic space where entrepreneurs don ornate masks, not to conceal but to reveal, not to hide but to accentuate.

Each mask is a narrative, an identity, a story intricately woven to resonate, to echo, to create ripples in the vast ocean of the market.

"Hide your designs, veil your strategies, let none decipher your intentions," echoed Sun-Tzu.

In the branding odyssey, this isn't an encouragement for opaqueness but a strategy of unveiling.

Each revelation is strategic, each unveiling choreographed, each revelation a calculated movement in the intricate dance of market dynamics.

The Audience's Ballet

In the realm of entrepreneurship, the audience isn't a passive entity but an active dancer.

Each step the brand takes, each movement it makes, is met with the audience's dance.

It's a silent yet eloquent ballet, a dance of shadows and lights, where the brand and audience are not separate entities but one harmonious existence.

In this dance, deception isn't trickery but artistry. It's a creative orchestration where the audience doesn't just witness the brand but experiences it, lives it, and breathes it.

The brand becomes a saga, an odyssey, an experience that transcends the tangible, echoing in the silent realms of perceptions, beliefs, and emotions.

Beyond the Veil

Entrepreneurs, armed with the silent echoes of Sun-Tzu's profound wisdom, venture beyond the veil.

Here, in the enigmatic spaces beyond tangible products and services, branding becomes an ethereal entity.

It's not a logo, a tagline, or a campaign, but a silent whisper, a mystical echo, a profound narrative that dwells, resonates, and echoes in the silent corridors of the audience's psyche.

The deception here isn't a concealment but an enhancement. It's an art where the unsaid is as potent as the said, the unseen as vivid as the seen, the unuttered as eloquent as the uttered.

Each silence is a narrative, each void a canvas where the audience paints its stories, weaves its perceptions, composes its symphonies.

Symphony of Sensations

Sun-Tzu's wisdom, *"Let your plans be dark and impenetrable as night, and when you move, fall like a thunderbolt,"* finds profound resonance in the realm of branding.

Each strategy is a silent night, a mystical expanse where plans are not just made but born, not just crafted but conceived, not just designed but destined.

When the brand moves, it's not just a step but a thunderbolt, not just a campaign but a revelation, not just a message but a symphony.

A symphony where each note is a sensation, each chord an emotion, each crescendo a climax of audience's profound engagement.

Resonating Echoes

As the chapter 'Deception: Branding and Marketing' spirals into its climax, the entrepreneur isn't just a business entity but a mystical presence, not just a competitor but a composer, not just a player but a poet.

In the silent scrolls of Sun-Tzu, the entrepreneur finds not strategies of warfare but melodies of branding, not tactics of conquest but harmonies of market enchantment.

In the intricate weave of deception, brands are not born but conjured, identities not made but destined, loyalties not built but ordained.

In the mystical spaces between Sun-Tzu's uttered wisdom and unuttered revelations, the brand and audience dance – not to the tunes of campaigns and strategies but to the silent, profound, mystical melodies of an odyssey where branding is not a tactic but a destiny, not a strategy but a soul's echo, not a plan but a profound, eternal, mystical dance of cosmic enchantment.

Each sentence woven, each word uttered, each silence embraced, unveils not a strategy but a narrative, not a plan but a journey, not a tactic but a saga – where Sun-Tzu's art of war and the modern entrepreneur's art of branding converge in a dance as ancient as time, as profound as silence, as mystical as the unuttered echoes of destiny's profound revelations.

The scrolls of Sun-Tzu, steeped in profound wisdom, become a silent scripture for the entrepreneur. Every line is a pathway, every word a stepping stone, and every silence a realm of profound discoveries.

In the mystical journey of branding, entrepreneurs don't just walk; they transcend, they don't just progress; they evolve, they don't just succeed; they transform.

The Canvas of Reality and Illusion

Sun-Tzu whispered, *"In conflict, direct confrontation will lead to engagement and surprise will lead to victory."*

The modern battlefield of business, echoing with the clashing titans of brands, resonates with this ancient whisper.
Entrepreneurs are not mere strategists; they are artists painting on the vast canvas where reality and illusion, clarity and mystery, engagement and surprise, dance in a celestial ballet.

The Echoes of Mystique

Branding is not a monologue of pronounced declarations; it is a silent dialogue of echoes and whispers, a dance of unveiling and veiling, revealing and concealing.

In this enigmatic dance, the brand emerges not as a static entity but a dynamic, breathing, living presence.

"Mystify, mislead, and surprise the enemy," said Sun-Tzu.

In the enigmatic corridors of the marketplace, this doesn't echo as a call for subterfuge but as an invitation to weave mystique, a charm, an enigmatic allure around the brand.

Each product, each service, each message, is imbued with a mystique that is as profound as it is captivating.

Brand - A Living Entity

In the heart of branding, the entrepreneur discovers that a brand is not a lifeless entity but a living organism.

It breathes, it pulses, it echoes with the vibrant rhythms of life. Each campaign is a breath, each message a heartbeat, each engagement a pulse echoing the vibrant dance of life.

Sun-Tzu's ancient landscapes of warriors and battlegrounds morph into a modern narrative where entrepreneurs are warriors, markets are battlegrounds, and branding is not a weapon but a living, breathing entity.

It's not wielded but embraced, not brandished but nurtured, not enforced but unveiled.

A Narrative of Soul

As the chapter 'Deception: Branding and Marketing' evolves, it unveils a narrative where soul and strategy converge, where art and war dance, where illusion and reality unite.

In the echoing corridors of Sun-Tzu's silent whispers and loud proclamations, entrepreneurs find not tactics but truths, not strategies but soul's echoes.

Every brand becomes a poem, every message a verse, every campaign a stanza in this epic poem where audience and brand, entrepreneur and market, message and silence, dance in a harmonious ballet - choreographed in the celestial spaces where Sun-Tzu's silent scrolls and modern entrepreneurship's loud narratives converge.

The Eternal Dance

The deception is not a trickery but a dance, not a subterfuge but an art, not a concealment but an unveiling.

Each veil lifted reveals a truth; each shadow cast unveils a light; each silence echoed pronounces a word of profound wisdom.

In the universe of 'Sun-Tzu's Art of War, Strategies for Modern Entrepreneurs', the dance of deception is not a battleground but a ballroom, not a conflict but a concert, not a war but a waltz.

Each step is grace, each move is art, each turn is a silent echo of a profound, eternal dance where war is not waged but transcended, battles not fought but danced, victories not claimed but composed.

Convergence of Echoes

As the dance spirals into an eternal crescendo, the entrepreneur, the brand, the audience, and Sun-Tzu become not separate dancers but one eternal entity, not distinct echoes but one profound sound, not isolated entities but one universal presence.

In the silent echoes of deception, branding is not a tactic but a hymn, not a strategy but a song, not a plan but a poem - echoing in the silent spaces where stars dance, galaxies waltz, and universes compose the eternal, silent, profound symphony of an entrepreneurial odyssey woven in the mystical threads of Sun-Tzu's silent, profound, eternal whispers.

Unfolding Horizons

In the mists of time, where ancient wisdom and modern innovation walk hand in hand, the deceptive art of branding and marketing reveals its true self - an odyssey of creation, a journey of revelation, and a dance of unison.

Every deception is a truth unveiled; every concealment, a revelation; every shadow, a light - in the eternal dance of business, where Sun-Tzu's warriors transform into modern entrepreneurs, and ancient battlegrounds morph into markets of boundless opportunities.

In this unfolding dance, the scrolls of Sun-Tzu aren't mere pages inked with wisdom but silent landscapes echoing with the untold stories, unuttered revelations, and unwritten symphonies of an entrepreneurial odyssey as profound as the cosmos, as mystical as the stars, and as eternal as the silent dance of galaxies in the uncharted terrains of the entrepreneurial universe.

Chapter 6:
Energy and Direction: Leading Teams

In the diverse and dynamic world of modern entrepreneurship, the echoes of Sun-Tzu's ancient wisdom provide a guiding light, illuminating pathways of leadership, team synergy, and organizational excellence.

This chapter, "Energy and Direction: Leading Teams," is a profound exploration into the harmonious convergence of ancient strategic wisdom and contemporary leadership paradigms.

The Nexus of Forces

Sun-Tzu professed the unity of forces, the harmonious integration of energies, to achieve supreme victory. For the modern entrepreneur, this unity is not an amalgamation of warriors but a synergy of diverse talents, skills, and abilities. Every team member is a unique energy, a distinct force, vibrating with the potential to contribute to the organization's unprecedented success.

"The supreme art of war is to subdue the enemy without fighting," Sun-Tzu declared.

In the contemporary entrepreneurial realm, this is not a confrontation with adversaries but an alignment of internal energies. The 'enemy' is not an external entity but internal discord, misalignment, and disharmony.

The Leadership Conduit

The entrepreneur, akin to the ancient general, becomes a conduit of energy. Each decision, each strategy, each directive, channels the team's diverse energies towards a singular direction, a united vision, a common goal.

Leadership is not authority but guidance, not command but inspiration, not control but empowerment.

The modern entrepreneur learns from Sun-Tzu that the battlefield's might is not in the clashing of swords but the unison of energies.

Every team member is a warrior, not of arms but of talents; every leader is a general, not of domination but of inspiration.

The Harmonious Battlefield

The battlefield transforms into an orchestration of harmonious energies, where leadership is a dance of guiding, channeling, and aligning diverse talents.

The leader is not an authoritarian figure but a maestro, orchestrating a symphony where each note is a team member's contribution, each chord a project's progression, each crescendo a milestone achievement.

"In the midst of chaos, there is also opportunity," Sun-Tzu professed. The chaos of diverse talents, multiple skills, and varied abilities is not a challenge but an opportunity - an opportunity to

weave a tapestry of organizational excellence where each thread is a team member's unique contribution.

Strategy and Soul

Sun-Tzu's strategies were soulful; they transcended the mechanics of warfare, delving into the artistry of human spirit, energy, and essence. For the modern entrepreneur, leading teams is a soulful art.

Each directive is infused with spirit; each decision, imbued with essence; each strategy, alive with energy.

Teams are not mechanical entities but soulful collectives, vibrating with the unseen yet palpable energies of human spirit, innovation, creativity, and collaboration.

The entrepreneur, guided by Sun-Tzu's wisdom, navigates this soulful terrain with the grace of a poet and the precision of a strategist.

Unleashing Potentials

"Energy may be likened to the bending of a crossbow; decision, to the releasing of a trigger," Sun-Tzu stated.

In this profound analogy, the modern interpretation for entrepreneurs lies in the bending as the harnessing of team energies, and the release as the strategic direction facilitating the unleashing of potentials.

Every team member is a bent crossbow, laden with untapped potentials. The entrepreneur's leadership is the trigger, releasing these pent-up energies to traverse the organizational landscapes, hitting targets of innovation, excellence, and success.

Navigating the Future

In the silent echoes of Sun-Tzu's ancient wisdom, the modern entrepreneur finds the melodies of future navigation. Teams are not static entities but dynamic forces; leadership is not a position but a journey; success is not a destination but an ongoing dance of energy, direction, unity, and harmony.

Concluding Rhapsody

As this chapter "Energy and Direction: Leading Teams" unveils its concluding notes, the melodies of Sun-Tzu's wisdom echo in the silent corridors of time, illuminating the pathways of modern entrepreneurs.

In this enlightened journey, enemies are not vanquished but energies harmonized; battles are not fought but potentials unleashed; victories are not claimed but visions realized.

In the symphony of Sun-Tzu's Art of War, the modern entrepreneur, the teams, the visions, and the energies, converge in a harmonious dance – a dance where the ancient wisdom of battlefields and the modern melodies of boardrooms, startups, and enterprises unite in a silent yet eloquent rhapsody of eternal resonance.

Chapter 7:

Weak Points and Strong: SWOT Analysis

In the ever-evolving battlefield of modern entrepreneurship, knowledge and foresight are your greatest allies.

Sun Tzu's ancient wisdom finds a contemporary counterpart in the form of strategic planning and analysis. One such tool that has become indispensable for entrepreneurs is the SWOT analysis.

In this chapter, we will explore how the principles of "Sun-Tzu's Art of War" can be effectively combined with SWOT analysis to assess your venture's Weak Points and Strong, offering you a roadmap to success in the competitive business world.

The Essence of SWOT Analysis

SWOT analysis is a strategic planning tool used to evaluate the Strengths, Weaknesses, Opportunities, and Threats of an organization or a project.

It provides a comprehensive overview of your current position in the market and helps you make informed decisions. Before we delve into the integration of Sun-Tzu's wisdom, let's break down the components of a SWOT analysis:

Strengths:

Strengths are the internal attributes that give your business an advantage over competitors. They could include factors such as a strong brand, unique product features, skilled workforce, or efficient processes.

Weaknesses:

Weaknesses are internal factors that hinder your business's performance or competitiveness. These could be issues like a lack of resources, outdated technology, poor management, or a limited product range.

Opportunities:

Opportunities are external factors in the market that can be leveraged to benefit your business. These could be emerging trends, new markets, changing consumer preferences, or technological advancements.

Threats:

Threats are external factors that could potentially harm your business. These might include competition, economic downturns, regulatory changes, or shifts in consumer behavior.

Sun-Tzu's Influence on SWOT Analysis

Sun-Tzu's "Art of War" teaches us to know ourselves and our enemies. This wisdom can be directly applied to SWOT analysis, where your business is both your ally and your adversary. Let's explore how Sun-Tzu's principles enhance each aspect of SWOT analysis:

Strengths: "Know Yourself"

Sun-Tzu emphasized the importance of knowing your own strengths and weaknesses. By aligning his wisdom with SWOT analysis, entrepreneurs can conduct a candid self-assessment. Identify your core competencies, the areas where you excel, and your unique selling propositions. Embrace these strengths and use them as the foundation for your strategy.

Sun-Tzu's counsel encourages you to leverage your strengths effectively, just as a skilled general would deploy their best troops in a crucial battle.

Weaknesses: "Know Your Enemy"

Sun-Tzu's directive to "know your enemy" translates seamlessly into understanding your weaknesses.

In the context of SWOT analysis, entrepreneurs must be brutally honest about their shortcomings.

Identifying weaknesses allows you to develop strategies for improvement or mitigation. Sun-Tzu's wisdom reminds us that acknowledging weaknesses is the first step toward turning them into strengths.

Opportunities: "Seize the Moment"

Sun-Tzu's advice to seize opportunities is perfectly aligned with the "Opportunities" section of SWOT analysis.

Once you've assessed your strengths and weaknesses, you can more effectively identify opportunities in the market.

Sun-Tzu encourages entrepreneurs to act swiftly and decisively, just as a wise commander seizes the right moment to strike. Use your insights to capitalize on emerging trends and market gaps.

Threats: "Plan for the Unpredictable"

Incorporating Sun-Tzu's philosophy into the "Threats" aspect of SWOT analysis encourages proactive planning. Sun-Tzu teaches us to be prepared for the unexpected, and this applies to identifying potential threats.

By foreseeing challenges and planning strategies to counter them, entrepreneurs can navigate turbulent times with greater resilience.

Applying Sun-Tzu's SWOT Analysis in Modern Entrepreneurship

The integration of Sun-Tzu's wisdom with SWOT analysis creates a powerful tool for modern entrepreneurs. Here's a step-by-step guide on how to apply this approach:

Step 1: Gather Your Troops

Assemble a team of key stakeholders and experts to conduct the SWOT analysis. Diverse perspectives can provide valuable insights.

Step 2: Know Thyself

Begin by assessing your internal strengths and weaknesses honestly. Analyze your resources, capabilities, and competitive advantages.

Step 3: Know Your Enemy

Examine your industry, competitors, and the external forces at play. Identify potential threats and challenges that could disrupt your business.

Step 4: Seize the Moment

Based on your strengths and opportunities, develop strategies to maximize your advantages in the market. Consider how you can capitalize on emerging trends.

Step 5: Plan for the Unpredictable

Create contingency plans for potential threats and weaknesses. Anticipate scenarios and develop responses to mitigate risks.

Step 6: Execute Your Strategy

Implement your strategy with precision, just as Sun-Tzu would execute a battle plan. Monitor your progress and be prepared to adapt as circumstances change.

In the dynamic world of modern entrepreneurship, combining Sun-Tzu's wisdom with the structured approach of SWOT analysis equips you with a formidable strategy.

By understanding your Weak Points and Strong, you can navigate the competitive landscape with confidence. Remember, just as a skilled general wins battles with strategic wisdom, so too can a modern entrepreneur conquer markets with the fusion of timeless insights and contemporary analysis.

As you apply Sun-Tzu's principles to your SWOT analysis, you will discover that your entrepreneurial journey becomes a battlefield of strategic brilliance, where you emerge as the victor in the ever-evolving world of business.

In this chapter, we've explored how Sun-Tzu's "Art of War" can enhance the effectiveness of SWOT analysis for modern entrepreneurs.

By integrating these principles, entrepreneurs can gain a deeper understanding of their businesses and develop strategies for success.

Chapter 8:
The Nine Situations: Business Models

In the world of modern entrepreneurship, where competition is fierce and markets are ever-evolving, entrepreneurs must adopt a multifaceted approach to thrive. Sun-Tzu's "Art of War" provides valuable insights into the concept of the Nine Situations, which can be effectively applied to different business models.

In this chapter, we will explore how these ancient strategic principles can guide modern entrepreneurs in selecting and adapting their business models to achieve success.

The Essence of the Nine Situations

Sun-Tzu's Nine Situations are a framework for understanding the dynamics of conflict and strategy. These situations represent various scenarios that a commander or strategist may encounter on the battlefield.

By studying and applying these situations, one can develop effective strategies to respond to different circumstances. Let's briefly examine each of the Nine Situations and how they relate to business:

1.   Dispersive Ground

Dispersive Ground represents a situation where your forces are scattered, making it challenging to control and coordinate them. In business, this can relate to a fragmented market with various competitors. Entrepreneurs must find ways to unify their efforts and create a cohesive presence.

2. Facile Ground

Facile Ground signifies a situation where your forces have the advantage of easy movement and flexibility. In business, this can be analogous to having a highly adaptable business model that can pivot quickly in response to market changes.

3. Contentious Ground

Contentious Ground represents a situation where you and your competitors are evenly matched, and neither side has a significant advantage. This situation mirrors industries with intense competition, requiring entrepreneurs to differentiate themselves and gain an edge.

4. Open Ground

Open Ground signifies a situation where you have a clear advantage, much like commanding the high ground on a battlefield. In business, this relates to having a unique value proposition or a dominant position in the market.

5. Ground of Intersecting Highways

Ground of Intersecting Highways represents a situation where different routes converge. In business, this can reflect opportunities to collaborate with other companies or enter strategic partnerships to expand your reach.

6. Serious Ground

Serious Ground signifies a situation where the stakes are high, and the outcome carries significant consequences. This relates to critical business decisions, such as entering new markets or launching innovative products, where careful planning is essential.

7. Difficult Ground

Difficult Ground represents challenging terrain that can impede your progress. In business, this can be akin to facing regulatory hurdles or navigating complex supply chains. Entrepreneurs must find ways to overcome obstacles effectively.

8. Hemmed-in Ground

Hemmed-in Ground is a situation where your options are limited due to external constraints. In business, this can be related to financial constraints or market saturation, requiring creative solutions to break free from limitations.

9. Desperate Ground

Desperate Ground represents a dire situation where the stakes are life and death. In business, this can symbolize a make-or-break moment, such as a financial crisis or a major product failure, where strategic decisions are critical for survival.

Applying the Nine Situations to Business Models

Now that we've explored the Nine Situations, let's delve into how these principles can guide entrepreneurs in selecting and adapting their business models:

Dispersive Ground Business Model

In industries with numerous competitors, like e-commerce, entrepreneurs can unify their efforts through partnerships, alliances, or niche targeting. Collaboration can help create a more cohesive market presence.

Facile Ground Business Model

Entrepreneurs in rapidly changing markets, such as technology, benefit from a facile ground model. They must build highly adaptable organizations capable of quick pivots to stay ahead of the curve.

Contentious Ground Business Model

In crowded markets, differentiation is key. Entrepreneurs must focus on creating unique value propositions, innovative solutions, or exceptional customer experiences to gain an advantage.

Open Ground Business Model

Having a dominant market position calls for strategies that maintain and strengthen that position, whether through continuous innovation, superior customer service, or expanding into adjacent markets.

Ground of Intersecting Highways Business Model

In this scenario, entrepreneurs can explore strategic collaborations, joint ventures, or partnerships to leverage the convergence of opportunities and expand their reach.

Serious Ground Business Model

High-stakes decisions require thorough market research, meticulous planning, and risk mitigation strategies. Entrepreneurs must weigh the potential rewards against the risks before proceeding.

Difficult Ground Business Model

Navigating challenging terrain demands creative problem-solving and resourceful thinking. Entrepreneurs must find innovative ways to overcome obstacles and keep moving forward.

Hemmed-in Ground Business Model

In situations where options are limited, entrepreneurs can seek external funding, strategic investors, or explore new markets to break free from constraints.

Desperate Ground Business Model

During make-or-break moments, entrepreneurs must be decisive and take calculated risks. These situations call for bold actions, potential restructuring, or pivoting to new business models for survival.

In the complex and dynamic world of modern entrepreneurship, the application of Sun-Tzu's Nine Situations to business models offers a strategic roadmap.

By understanding these situations and selecting the most appropriate business model, entrepreneurs can navigate the challenges and opportunities of their respective industries with wisdom and foresight.

Remember that the key to success lies not only in selecting the right business model but also in adapting it as circumstances change. Just as a wise commander adjusts strategies on the battlefield, modern entrepreneurs must be agile and responsive to maintain their competitive edge in the ever-evolving world of business.

Incorporating the principles of the Nine Situations into your business model decisions can lead to strategic brilliance and victory in the marketplace.

In this chapter, we've explored how Sun-Tzu's Nine Situations can be applied to different business models, offering entrepreneurs a strategic framework to make informed decisions and adapt to changing circumstances.

Chapter 9:

Attacking by Stratagem: Market Disruption

In the fiercely competitive landscape of modern entrepreneurship, market disruption is not just a buzzword; it's a strategic imperative.

Sun-Tzu's "Art of War" offers profound insights into the art of attacking by stratagem, and this chapter explores how these principles can be applied to disrupt markets and gain a competitive advantage in the digital age.

The Essence of Market Disruption

Market disruption is a strategy that aims to overthrow established market leaders by introducing innovative products, services, or business models that fundamentally change the industry's dynamics. It involves identifying weaknesses in the existing market structure and capitalizing on them to create a new playing field. Let's dive into the key components of market disruption:

1. Identifying Vulnerabilities:

Market disruptors keenly observe the weaknesses in the status quo. They look for areas where incumbents are complacent, inefficient, or overlooking emerging trends.

2. Innovation:

Innovation is at the heart of market disruption. Disruptors develop groundbreaking solutions that address the identified vulnerabilities, offering something radically different from existing offerings.

3. Customer-Centric Approach:

Disruptors prioritize the needs and preferences of their target customers. They aim to provide a superior customer experience that incumbent players fail to deliver.

4. Nimble Execution:

Market disruptors execute their strategies swiftly and with precision. They are agile, able to adapt to changing circumstances, and make rapid adjustments to their business models.

5. Sustainable Growth:

Successful market disruptors not only introduce innovations but also build sustainable growth models that allow them to scale and dominate their markets.

Sun-Tzu's strategic wisdom is a valuable guide for entrepreneurs seeking to disrupt markets effectively:

Attack by Stratagem:

Sun-Tzu advocated attacking by stratagem, emphasizing the importance of surprise, speed, and calculated moves. In the context of market disruption, this means launching innovative products or services when competitors least expect it, taking them off guard.

Know the Terrain:

Understanding the terrain was paramount for Sun-Tzu. In modern entrepreneurship, knowing the market landscape is equally crucial. Disruptors must research their industry thoroughly, identify gaps, and leverage this knowledge to navigate market dynamics effectively.

Deception and Misdirection:

Sun-Tzu's teachings on deception are applicable in market disruption. Entrepreneurs can create a diversion by focusing competitors' attention on one area while secretly working on a disruptive innovation in another.

Exploiting Weaknesses:

Sun-Tzu's emphasis on exploiting the enemy's weaknesses aligns with the concept of identifying vulnerabilities in market disruption. Disruptors seek opportunities where competitors are weak, providing an opening to gain a competitive edge.

Applying Sun-Tzu's Wisdom to Market Disruption

Now, let's explore how modern entrepreneurs can apply Sun-Tzu's principles to execute market disruption successfully:

Identify Market Gaps:

Thoroughly analyze your industry to identify unmet needs, pain points, or areas where incumbent players are falling short. This forms the foundation of your disruption strategy.

Innovation is Key:

Embrace innovation as a means of gaining a strategic advantage. Develop disruptive products or services that challenge the status quo and offer a superior solution to existing problems.

Customer Focus

Prioritize your customers. Understand their needs, desires, and pain points, and design your offerings to provide exceptional value and a seamless experience.

Speed and Precision:

Execute your market disruption strategy swiftly and with precision. Minimize delays, bureaucracy, and unnecessary processes that can hinder innovation.

Scalability:

Ensure that your disruption model is scalable. As your business gains traction, be prepared to expand rapidly while maintaining the same level of innovation and customer focus.

Long-Term Vision:

Market disruption is not a one-time event but a long-term strategy. Have a clear vision for the future and continuously innovate to maintain your disruptive edge.

Case Studies of Market Disruption

Uber

Uber disrupted the traditional taxi industry by leveraging technology to create a more convenient and efficient ride-sharing platform. They identified vulnerabilities in the taxi market, such as unreliable service and payment methods, and addressed them with a disruptive solution.

Airbnb

Airbnb disrupted the hotel industry by connecting travelers with unique and affordable accommodations. They capitalized on the underutilization of spare rooms and properties, offering a new experience for travelers worldwide.

Tesla

Tesla disrupted the automotive industry by introducing electric vehicles with cutting-edge technology and sustainability in mind. They recognized the need for cleaner transportation and shifted the paradigm of the automotive market.

Netflix

Netflix disrupted the entertainment industry by transitioning from DVD rentals to online streaming. They recognized the shift in consumer behavior and preferences, offering a more flexible and convenient way to access content.

Market disruption is not reserved for tech giants alone. Sun-Tzu's timeless wisdom teaches us that with strategic planning, innovation, and customer-centric approaches, any entrepreneur can embark on a journey to disrupt markets and create a lasting impact.

By understanding the vulnerabilities in existing market structures and capitalizing on them with innovative solutions, modern entrepreneurs can follow in the footsteps of industry disruptors and rewrite the rules of their respective markets.

Remember that successful market disruption is not about merely introducing a new product; it's about fundamentally changing the way an industry operates.

It's about leveraging Sun-Tzu's principles of strategy and surprise to attack by stratagem, ultimately achieving victory in the battle for market dominance.

In the dynamic world of modern entrepreneurship, embracing the art of market disruption can propel you to the forefront of your industry, reshaping the competitive landscape and paving the way for innovation and progress.

The Art of Disruptive Innovation

Disruptive innovation, a term popularized by Harvard Business School professor Clayton Christensen, refers to innovations that create new markets or significantly alter existing ones. These innovations often start by serving smaller, overlooked segments of the market but gradually evolve to challenge and surpass established players.

The Role of Technology

Technology plays a pivotal role in many disruptive innovations. Entrepreneurs leverage technological advancements to introduce new and efficient ways of doing things. Whether it's the internet, mobile apps, or advanced data analytics, technology can be a powerful enabler of market disruption.

The Disruptor's Dilemma

Disruptors face what Christensen called the "Innovator's Dilemma." Established companies tend to focus on improving their existing products and serving their current customers, making it challenging to invest in disruptive innovations. This creates an opportunity for agile startups to enter the market with fresh ideas and approaches.

Lessons from Disruptors

Let's take a closer look at some key lessons from successful market disruptors:

1. Customer-Centricity:

Disruptors prioritize understanding their customers deeply. They listen to their pain points, preferences, and desires and build solutions tailored to meet those needs better than existing options.

2. Agility and Flexibility:

Successful disruptors are agile and can pivot quickly based on market feedback. They aren't tied down by bureaucratic processes or legacy systems, allowing them to adapt to changing circumstances.

3. Data-Driven Decision-Making:

Data is a disruptor's best friend. They leverage data analytics to make informed decisions, refine their offerings, and identify growth opportunities.

Data provides insights into customer behavior and market trends.

4. Risk-Taking:

Market disruption often involves calculated risk-taking. Disruptors are willing to challenge the status quo, even if it means facing initial resistance. They understand that innovation inherently involves uncertainty.

5. Long-Term Vision:

Successful disruptors have a clear long-term vision. They don't aim for short-term gains but rather focus on creating lasting impacts and reshaping industries over time.

Embracing Market Disruption

Aspiring entrepreneurs can embrace the principles of market disruption by following these steps:

1.   Identify Market Gaps:

Conduct thorough market research to identify gaps and inefficiencies within your industry. Look for areas where customer needs are not being fully met or where technology can be harnessed for improvement.

2. Innovate Fearlessly:

Don't be afraid to challenge conventional wisdom and embrace innovation. Consider how emerging technologies or new business models can be leveraged to create value and improve upon existing solutions.

3. Prioritize Customer Experience:

Place your customers at the center of your strategy. Understand their pain points, gather feedback, and continuously strive to enhance their experience with your product or service.

4. Stay Agile:

Maintain agility in your organization. Be prepared to pivot, iterate, and adapt to changing market conditions. Avoid getting locked into rigid structures that hinder innovation.

5. Leverage Data:

Collect and analyze data to inform your decisions. Use data-driven insights to refine your strategies, identify growth opportunities, and track your progress.

6. Be Resilient:

Market disruption can be challenging, and setbacks are likely along the way. Stay resilient, learn from failures, and keep your long-term vision in focus.

Conclusion: The Path to Market Disruption

Market disruption is not reserved for a select few; it's a strategic approach that any entrepreneur can adopt. By aligning with Sun-Tzu's principles of strategy and surprise and by embracing the lessons from successful disruptors, you can embark on a journey to disrupt markets and create a lasting impact.

In the dynamic world of modern entrepreneurship, market disruption represents not only a strategic imperative but also an opportunity to reshape industries, drive innovation, and elevate your business to new heights.

The art of market disruption is not just about winning market share; it's about rewriting the rules of the game and leading the charge toward progress and transformation.

As you navigate the complexities of market disruption, remember that with innovation, customer-centricity, and a long-term vision, you have the potential to not only succeed but to become a force that reshapes the competitive landscape and inspires others to innovate and challenge the status quo.

Market disruption is a dynamic and evolving field, and successful disruptors continue to reshape industries worldwide. If you'd like to delve further into specific aspects or explore case studies of disruptive companies, please feel free to ask for more information or insights on any topic of interest.

In this chapter, we've explored how Sun-Tzu's principles can be applied to the concept of market disruption, offering modern entrepreneurs a strategic framework to challenge established norms and gain a competitive edge.

Chapter 10:

Passive and Active Strategy: The Pivot

In the ever-shifting landscape of modern entrepreneurship, adaptability is not just a virtue; it's a survival strategy. Sun-Tzu's "Art of War" provides profound insights into the art of pivoting, a strategic maneuver that allows businesses to navigate changing circumstances, seize opportunities, and overcome challenges.

In this chapter, we will explore the concepts of passive and active strategies and how the pivot serves as a dynamic tool for modern entrepreneurs.

The Essence of the Pivot

The pivot is a strategic shift in a company's direction, typically in response to changes in the market, customer feedback, or evolving business conditions.
It involves altering the business model, product offerings, or target audience to better align with emerging opportunities or to address unexpected challenges.
The pivot can be either passive or active, depending on the nature and timing of the change.

Passive Pivot:

A passive pivot occurs in response to external forces or market pressures that necessitate a change in strategy. This might involve adjusting pricing, modifying product features, or repositioning the brand to stay competitive. Passive pivots are often reactive and driven by the need to survive in a changing environment.

Active Pivot:

An active pivot, on the other hand, is a proactive strategic shift driven by a desire to capitalize on new opportunities or to stay ahead of evolving trends. Entrepreneurs who actively pivot are visionary leaders who anticipate changes in the market and are willing to make bold moves to maintain a competitive edge.

Sun-Tzu's Influence on the Pivot

Sun-Tzu's principles of strategy and adaptation are closely tied to the concept of the pivot:

<u>The Importance of Flexibility:</u>

Sun-Tzu emphasized the importance of being flexible in the face of changing circumstances. He advised that the victorious strategist is one who can adapt and adjust to the ever-evolving nature of warfare. This principle directly applies to entrepreneurs facing the challenges of the business world.

<u>Timing and Opportunity:</u>

Sun-Tzu's teachings underscored the significance of timing and recognizing opportunities. Entrepreneurs who actively pivot are like astute commanders who seize the right moment to change direction and gain an advantage.

Deception and Misdirection:

Sun-Tzu's wisdom regarding deception and misdirection can also be applied to the pivot. Entrepreneurs may strategically pivot without revealing their full intentions to competitors, creating an element of surprise.

Passive Pivots: Adapting to External Pressures

Passive pivots are often a response to external pressures or market changes. Here are some common scenarios in which passive pivots may be necessary:

Competitive Threats:

When new competitors enter the market or existing ones gain a significant advantage, businesses may need to passively pivot to strengthen their competitive position. This could involve adjusting pricing, enhancing product features, or improving customer service.

Economic Downturns:

During economic recessions or downturns, consumer behavior and spending patterns may change. Businesses may need to passively pivot by diversifying their product offerings, expanding into new markets, or implementing cost-cutting measures to weather the economic storm.

Regulatory Changes:

Changes in government regulations can have a profound impact on certain industries. Businesses affected by regulatory shifts may need to passively pivot by ensuring compliance, altering their business models, or lobbying for favorable changes.

Technological Advancements:

Rapid technological advancements can render existing products or services obsolete. To remain relevant, businesses may need to passively pivot by investing in research and development, embracing new technologies, or reshaping their product lines.

Active Pivots: Proactively Seizing Opportunities

Active pivots involve proactive shifts in strategy to seize emerging opportunities or stay ahead of the curve. Entrepreneurs who actively pivot are visionary leaders who understand the value of agility and innovation. Here are some scenarios where active pivots can be highly effective:

Market Expansion:

Entrepreneurs may actively pivot by expanding into new markets or geographic regions where untapped opportunities exist. This might involve customizing products or services to cater to the unique needs of different customer segments.

Product Innovation:

Innovation is a driving force behind active pivots. Entrepreneurs can proactively pivot by investing in research and development to create innovative products or services that disrupt existing markets or create entirely new ones.

Business Model Transformation:

Entrepreneurs who anticipate shifts in consumer behavior or industry trends may proactively pivot by transforming their business models. For example, moving from a traditional brick-and-mortar retail model to an e-commerce platform.

Strategic Partnerships:

Active pivots can also involve forming strategic partnerships or alliances with other companies. Collaborative ventures can help businesses access new markets, technologies, or distribution channels.

The Pivot as a Continuous Process

Successful entrepreneurs understand that the pivot is not a one-time event but a continuous process. To embrace the pivot as a strategic tool, consider the following steps:

1. Constant Monitoring:

Stay vigilant and monitor the external landscape. Keep an eye on market trends, customer feedback, and emerging opportunities or threats.

2. Risk Assessment:

Evaluate the potential risks and rewards of pivoting. Consider the impact on your business, customers, and competitors.

3. Strategic Planning:

Develop a clear strategy for the pivot, whether it's passive or active. Outline the steps, resources, and timeline required for successful execution.

4. Implementation:

Execute the pivot with precision and agility. Communicate changes to stakeholders, and ensure your team is aligned with the new strategy.

5. Feedback and Iteration:

Gather feedback from customers, employees, and other stakeholders. Use this input to refine your strategy and make necessary adjustments. The pivot is an iterative process that may require fine-tuning based on real-world feedback.

6. Measuring Success:

Establish key performance indicators (KPIs) to measure the success of the pivot. Determine whether the changes are achieving the desired outcomes and aligning with your long-term goals.

7. Adaptability:

Maintain a culture of adaptability within your organization. Encourage employees to embrace change, provide opportunities for professional development, and foster a mindset that values innovation and continuous improvement.

Case Studies of Successful Pivots

Let's examine a few notable case studies of companies that effectively utilized both passive and active pivots to navigate changing circumstances and achieve success:

Netflix: From DVD Rentals to Streaming Giant (Active Pivot)

Netflix initially began as a DVD rental service but recognized the shift in consumer behavior toward online streaming.

They actively pivoted by investing heavily in digital streaming technology and transitioning their business model. Today, Netflix is a global streaming powerhouse.

Apple: From Personal Computers to Consumer Electronics (Active Pivot)

Apple started as a computer company but later pivoted to become a leader in consumer electronics, launching iconic products like the iPhone and iPad.

This active pivot involved diversifying their product portfolio and entering new markets.

Twitter: From Podcasting to Microblogging (Passive Pivot)

Twitter originally focused on podcasting but observed that users were more interested in short text updates.

They passively pivoted by shifting their emphasis to microblogging, which ultimately led to the creation of one of the most influential social media platforms in the world.

IBM: From Hardware to Services (Active Pivot)

IBM was known for its hardware products but recognized the declining demand for hardware and the growing importance of software and services.

They proactively pivoted by shifting their focus to software and services, becoming a leading IT solutions provider.

Instagram: From Location-Based Check-In to Photo Sharing (Active Pivot)

Instagram initially started as a location-based check-in app but realized that users were primarily interested in sharing photos.

They actively pivoted by refocusing their platform on photo sharing, leading to explosive growth and acquisition by Facebook.

Conclusion: Embracing the Pivot

In the dynamic and unpredictable world of modern entrepreneurship, the pivot is not a sign of weakness but a testament to adaptability and strategic thinking. Sun-Tzu's principles of flexibility, timing, and seizing opportunities resonate deeply with the art of the pivot.

Whether you find yourself reacting to external pressures or proactively seeking new opportunities, the pivot is a strategic tool that empowers entrepreneurs to navigate change, evolve their businesses, and achieve success.

By embracing both passive and active pivots, entrepreneurs can master the art of adaptability and remain at the forefront of innovation.

As you embark on your entrepreneurial journey, remember that the ability to pivot is not just a survival skill; it's a competitive advantage that can propel your business to new heights.

Continuously monitor the landscape, assess risks and opportunities, and be willing to make bold moves when necessary. In doing so, you can navigate the ever-evolving battlefield of modern entrepreneurship with wisdom, agility, and strategic brilliance.

In this chapter, we've explored the concepts of passive and active pivots as strategic maneuvers for modern entrepreneurs.

Chapter 11:
The Use of Spies: Competitive Analysis

In the world of modern entrepreneurship, where competition is fierce and market dynamics are constantly evolving, the ability to gather intelligence and conduct competitive analysis is paramount.

Sun-Tzu's "Art of War" offers valuable insights into the use of spies as a strategic tool, and in this chapter, we will explore how these principles can be applied by modern entrepreneurs for competitive advantage.

The Role of Competitive Analysis

Competitive analysis involves the systematic examination of your competitors, their strengths, weaknesses, strategies, and market positioning. This process provides valuable intelligence that can inform your own business strategies, helping you make informed decisions, identify opportunities, and mitigate threats.

Let's delve into the key components of competitive analysis and how it aligns with Sun-Tzu's teachings.

1.   Know Your Competitors:

To effectively compete in any market, you must first identify and understand your competitors. This includes both direct competitors who offer similar products or services and indirect competitors who may meet similar customer needs through different means.

2. Strengths and Weaknesses:

Sun-Tzu emphasized the importance of knowing your enemy as well as yourself. In competitive analysis, this translates to identifying the strengths and weaknesses of your competitors.

Recognizing their advantages can help you find ways to counter them, while understanding their vulnerabilities allows you to exploit opportunities.

3. Strategies and Tactics:

Just as generals study the tactics of their adversaries, entrepreneurs must analyze the strategies and tactics employed by competitors. This includes examining their marketing approaches, pricing strategies, customer engagement methods, and more.

4. Market Positioning:

Understanding where your competitors stand in the market is crucial. Are they market leaders, challengers, or niche players? Knowing their positioning can help you determine where your business fits and how to differentiate yourself.

5. Customer Insights:

Competitive analysis often includes gathering customer feedback and insights related to your competitors. What do customers like or dislike about their products or services? This information can guide your own product development and customer service efforts.

6. Market Trends and Opportunities:

By monitoring your competitors, you can also stay attuned to broader market trends and emerging opportunities. Recognizing shifts in consumer behavior or industry dynamics can help you adjust your strategies accordingly.

The Use of Spies: Sun-Tzu's Strategic Wisdom

Sun-Tzu's teachings on the use of spies are highly relevant to competitive analysis in modern entrepreneurship:

Covert Information Gathering:

In "The Art of War," spies are used to gather critical information about the enemy's plans and intentions discreetly. In the business world, this can be equated to market research and competitive intelligence.

It involves collecting data on competitors without their knowledge, which can include studying their online presence, analyzing financial reports, and even attending industry events to observe their activities.

Deception and Misdirection:

Sun-Tzu's teachings on deception can be applied to competitive analysis. Just as spies may use deception to conceal their true intentions, businesses can employ tactics to mislead competitors, such as launching a fake product or service to gauge the competition's reaction.

Predicting Competitor Actions:

Sun-Tzu advised using spies to anticipate the enemy's moves. In the business world, this means studying competitors' behaviors and past actions to predict their future strategies. For example, if a competitor has a history of aggressive price cuts, you can anticipate similar moves and prepare accordingly.

Understanding Motivations:

Sun-Tzu suggested that spies should understand the motivations and mindset of the enemy. In competitive analysis, this translates to deciphering the underlying motivations behind your competitors' actions. Are they driven by market share, profitability, innovation, or market domination? Understanding their motivations can help you respond effectively.

Conducting Effective Competitive Analysis

Now, let's explore the steps for conducting effective competitive analysis in the context of modern entrepreneurship:

1. Identify Competitors:

Begin by creating a list of your key competitors. Consider both direct and indirect competitors who operate in your industry or cater to a similar target audience.

2. Gather Information:

Collect as much information as possible about your competitors. This may include their product offerings, pricing strategies, market share, financial performance, customer reviews, and public statements.

3. Analyze Strengths and Weaknesses:

Evaluate the strengths and weaknesses of each competitor. Identify their unique selling points, competitive advantages, and areas where they may be vulnerable.

4. Study Strategies and Tactics:

Examine the strategies and tactics employed by your competitors. This includes their marketing campaigns, customer acquisition methods, distribution channels, and partnerships.

5. Assess Market Positioning:

Determine where your competitors stand in the market. Are they leaders in a specific niche, challengers trying to disrupt the status quo, or followers trying to catch up?

6. Collect Customer Insights:

Gather customer feedback and insights related to your competitors. Online reviews, surveys, and social media discussions can provide valuable information about customer satisfaction and pain points.

7. Monitor Market Trends:

Stay updated on industry trends and emerging opportunities. Understanding the broader market landscape can help you position your business strategically.

Applying Competitive Analysis: A Case Study
Let's explore how competitive analysis can be applied using a fictional case study:

Scenario: Imagine you run a small e-commerce business specializing in handmade jewelry. You've identified two main competitors in your niche: "EcoGems" and "ArtisanJewels."

Competitive Analysis:

- Identifying Competitors:

    - EcoGems and ArtisanJewels are direct competitors offering handmade jewelry products.

- Gathering Information:

    - Research their websites, product catalogs, and pricing structures.
    - Analyze their social media presence, customer reviews, and online advertising efforts.
    - Study their financial reports (if available) to gauge their financial stability and growth.

- Analyzing Strengths and Weaknesses:

  - EcoGems specializes in eco-friendly materials, which appeals to environmentally conscious consumers. However, they have limited product variety.

  - ArtisanJewels offers a wide range of unique designs but has received mixed customer reviews regarding product quality.

- Studying Strategies and Tactics:

  - EcoGems runs social media campaigns emphasizing sustainability.

  - ArtisanJewels frequently introduces new designs and offers seasonal discounts.

- Assessing Market Positioning:

  - EcoGems positions itself as a leader in sustainable jewelry.

- ArtisanJewels aims to attract a broader audience with its diverse product range.

- Collecting Customer Insights:

  - Review customer feedback on their websites and social media.

  - Conduct surveys to gather opinions on what customers value most in handmade jewelry.

- Monitoring Market Trends:

  - Stay updated on jewelry industry trends, such as rising demand for sustainable materials or shifts in design preferences.

Leveraging Competitive Analysis for Strategic Advantage

Competitive analysis is not a one-time task but an ongoing process. By continually monitoring your competitors and adapting your strategies based on insights gained, you can position your business strategically and respond effectively to changes in the market.

1.   Identify Differentiation Opportunities:

Use the insights from your competitive analysis to identify opportunities for differentiation. Is there a gap in the market that your competitors have overlooked? Can you capitalize on their weaknesses or offer a unique value proposition?

2. Refine Your Marketing Strategy:

Tailor your marketing campaigns based on what you've learned about your competitors' tactics. Highlight your strengths and address your customers' pain points more effectively than your rivals.

3. Adjust Pricing Strategies:

If you've identified that your competitors use aggressive pricing as a key strategy, consider your pricing approach. You may choose to compete on value, quality, or unique features rather than engaging in a price war.

4. Customer Engagement and Experience:

Use customer insights gathered from competitive analysis to enhance your own customer engagement and experience. Address the areas where your competitors may be falling short and exceed customer expectations.

5. Innovation and Product Development:

Innovation is a powerful tool for gaining a competitive edge. Use your understanding of market trends and your competitors' weaknesses to drive innovation in your products or services.

6. Strategic Partnerships:

Consider forming strategic partnerships or collaborations with businesses that can complement your offerings and help you compete more effectively in the market.

7. Anticipate Competitive Moves:

Continuously monitor your competitors to anticipate their next moves. This proactive approach can give you a head start in responding to their strategies.

8. Track Your Progress:

Regularly measure the impact of your strategies and adjustments. Are you gaining market share?

Are customers responding positively? Use metrics and KPIs to track your progress.

The Ethical Consideration

While competitive analysis is a valuable tool for business growth, it's essential to conduct it ethically and within legal boundaries. Avoid any unethical practices, such as corporate espionage or unfair competition. Respect privacy laws and intellectual property rights.

Conclusion: The Competitive Edge

In the relentless pursuit of success in modern entrepreneurship, competitive analysis is your secret weapon. Just as Sun-Tzu's spies provided invaluable intelligence for strategic advantage, your thorough understanding of competitors can guide your decisions and help you stay one step ahead.

Remember that competitive analysis is not about imitation but about innovation. It's about leveraging insights to differentiate your business, enhance customer value, and ultimately achieve a sustainable competitive edge.

By embracing the principles of competitive analysis and consistently applying them, you can navigate the competitive landscape with confidence, make informed decisions, and position your business for long-term success.

Competitive Analysis in Action

To gain a deeper understanding of how competitive analysis can be applied in the real world, let's consider a practical example within the context of modern entrepreneurship.

Scenario: Imagine you own a small software development company specializing in mobile app development. Two of your main competitors in this space are "TechApps Inc." and "InnoTech Solutions."
Competitive Analysis in Action:

- Identifying Competitors:

    - TechApps Inc. and InnoTech Solutions are your direct competitors, offering similar mobile app development services.

- Gathering Information:

  - Analyze their websites, client portfolios, and case studies to gain insights into the types of apps they develop and their expertise.

  - Monitor their social media channels and blog posts to learn about their latest projects and industry insights.

  - Review online customer reviews and ratings to understand client satisfaction levels.

- Analyzing Strengths and Weaknesses:

  - TechApps Inc. is known for its expertise in gaming app development but has limited experience in business and productivity apps.

  - InnoTech Solutions has a strong track record in enterprise app development but may lack the creativity seen in TechApps Inc.'s gaming apps.

- Studying Strategies and Tactics:

  - TechApps Inc. frequently runs social media campaigns targeting the gaming community and sponsors gaming events.

  - InnoTech Solutions focuses on B2B marketing, attending industry trade shows and hosting webinars for enterprise clients.

- Assessing Market Positioning:

  - TechApps Inc. is positioned as an innovative leader in the gaming app sector.

  - InnoTech Solutions positions itself as a reliable partner for businesses seeking enterprise-level mobile solutions.

- Collecting Customer Insights:

  - Analyze customer reviews to identify common pain points and areas where competitors may fall short in meeting client expectations.

- Conduct surveys or interviews with potential clients to understand what factors influence their choice of mobile app development partner.

- Monitoring Market Trends:

  - Stay updated on emerging trends in mobile app development, such as the rise of augmented reality (AR) apps or the increasing demand for security features in enterprise apps.

Leveraging Competitive Insights

Now, let's explore how you can leverage the insights gained from competitive analysis to strengthen your position in the market:ù

1. Niche Specialization:

Based on your analysis, you could consider specializing in a niche where your competitors have weaknesses. For example, if TechApps Inc. lacks experience in business apps, you could position your company as a specialist in this area.

2. Tailored Marketing:

Craft marketing campaigns that resonate with your target audience. If your research indicates that enterprise clients value reliability and security, emphasize these aspects in your messaging.

3. Innovation:

Use your understanding of market trends to innovate and offer cutting-edge features or technologies in your app development projects. This can set you apart as an industry innovator.

4. Strategic Partnerships:

Consider forming strategic partnerships with businesses that complement your strengths. For instance, collaborating with a design agency can enhance the aesthetics of your apps.

5. Customer-Centric Approach:

Address the pain points identified in customer reviews and surveys. Prioritize customer satisfaction and actively seek feedback to continuously improve your services.

6. Track Competitor Movements:

Keep a watchful eye on your competitors' actions. If TechApps Inc. starts expanding into business app development, be prepared to adjust your strategies accordingly.

7. Adapt to Trends:

Stay agile and adapt to emerging trends. If AR apps become popular, invest in the necessary skills and technology to offer AR development services.

Ethical Considerations

As you leverage competitive insights, always uphold ethical standards. Avoid engaging in practices that could harm your competitors or violate industry regulations. Ethical conduct is not only a moral imperative but also essential for maintaining a positive industry reputation.

Conclusion: A Competitive Advantage

Competitive analysis is a dynamic process that empowers entrepreneurs with valuable insights and strategic advantages. By applying the principles of understanding, differentiation, and adaptability, you can navigate the competitive landscape effectively and position your business for success.

In the ever-evolving world of modern entrepreneurship, the ability to gather intelligence, adapt to changing circumstances, and make informed decisions is the key to gaining a competitive edge.

As you continue your entrepreneurial journey, remember that the art of competitive analysis is not about merely keeping up with the competition; it's about staying ahead and leading the way in your industry.

By embracing the wisdom of Sun-Tzu and continuously honing your competitive analysis skills, you can chart a course towards sustained growth, innovation, and excellence in the world of modern entrepreneurship.

In this chapter, we've explored competitive analysis as a strategic tool for modern entrepreneurs, providing practical insights and applications.

Chapter 12:

On Fire: Maintaining Passion and Determination

In the high-stakes world of modern entrepreneurship, passion and determination are the driving forces that ignite the entrepreneurial spirit.

Sun-Tzu's "Art of War" may seem an unlikely source of inspiration for such qualities, but the principles within its ancient wisdom can serve as a beacon for today's entrepreneurs seeking to maintain their fire and unwavering determination.

The Entrepreneurial Flame

Starting a business is often fueled by a burning passion, a vision that ignites a fire within the entrepreneur. This passion is the spark that propels individuals to take risks, overcome obstacles, and work tirelessly to bring their dreams to life. However, maintaining this flame in the face of adversity and the challenges of modern entrepreneurship can be a daunting task.

The Importance of Passion:

Passion is the emotional energy that fuels an entrepreneur's commitment to their vision. It provides the motivation to weather the storms, the resilience to bounce back from failures, and the creativity to find innovative solutions.

The Role of Determination:

Determination is the unwavering resolve to pursue one's goals despite setbacks and obstacles. It is the mental fortitude that keeps entrepreneurs focused on their mission and willing to put in the hard work required for success.

Sun-Tzu's Wisdom: A Source of Inspiration

While "The Art of War" primarily focuses on military strategy, its principles can be applied metaphorically to the battlefield of entrepreneurship:

1.   Know Yourself:

Sun-Tzu emphasized the importance of self-awareness. For entrepreneurs, this means understanding their passions, strengths, and values. Knowing what truly drives them can help maintain their fire.

2. Adaptability:

Sun-Tzu's teachings stress adaptability, the ability to adjust strategies in response to changing circumstances. Entrepreneurs must adapt to market shifts while staying true to their core passion and vision.

3. Resilience:

Sun-Tzu recognized the value of resilience in the face of adversity. Entrepreneurs, too, must be resilient to persevere through failures, setbacks, and the inevitable challenges of business.

4. Strategy and Planning:

Sun-Tzu's focus on strategy aligns with the need for entrepreneurs to have a clear plan. Having a well-thought-out strategy can provide direction and maintain the flame by setting achievable milestones.

5. Leadership:

Sun-Tzu emphasized the role of leadership in achieving victory. Entrepreneurs must be effective leaders, inspiring and motivating their teams to share their passion and determination.

The Entrepreneurial Journey

The entrepreneurial journey is often a rollercoaster ride filled with highs and lows. To maintain your passion and determination, consider the following strategies:

1. Reconnect with Your Why:

Reflect on why you started your entrepreneurial journey. What was the driving force behind your business idea? Reconnecting with your "why" can reignite your passion.

2. Set Meaningful Goals:

Establish clear and meaningful goals that align with your vision. Break them down into achievable steps, and celebrate each small victory along the way.

3. Embrace Challenges:

Rather than viewing challenges as obstacles, see them as opportunities for growth. Overcoming difficulties can reignite your determination as you prove your resilience.

4. Stay Inspired:

Continuously seek inspiration from various sources, whether it's reading books, attending conferences, or connecting with like-minded entrepreneurs. Inspiration can fuel your passion.

5. Practice Self-Care:

Maintaining your fire requires a healthy body and mind. Prioritize self-care, including exercise, meditation, and adequate rest, to keep your energy levels high.

6. Surround Yourself with Support:

Build a support network of mentors, advisors, and fellow entrepreneurs who understand your journey. They can provide guidance, encouragement, and a sense of camaraderie.

7. Celebrate Milestones:

Acknowledge and celebrate your achievements, no matter how small. Recognizing your progress can boost your determination and keep your passion burning.

8. Keep Learning:

Stay curious and continue learning. New knowledge and skills can invigorate your passion and help you adapt to evolving market dynamics.

Passion and Determination in Action

Let's explore a real-world example of how passion and determination have fueled an entrepreneur's success:

Case Study: Elon Musk, CEO of SpaceX and Tesla

Elon Musk's journey is a testament to unwavering passion and determination. He founded SpaceX with the goal of reducing space transportation costs to enable the colonization of Mars.

Despite numerous setbacks and failures, including multiple rocket launch failures, Musk remained resolute in his mission.

Musk's passion for sustainable transportation led him to establish Tesla, a company dedicated to accelerating the world's transition to electric vehicles.

Despite skepticism and challenges in the automotive industry, Musk's determination to combat climate change drove him to revolutionize the electric car market.

The Eternal Flame

Passion and determination are the lifeblood of entrepreneurship. They are the forces that drive entrepreneurs to take risks, innovate, and persevere in the face of adversity.

While the path of entrepreneurship is filled with challenges and uncertainties, the flame of passion and determination can illuminate the way forward.

As modern entrepreneurs, you are the torchbearers of innovation and progress.

Sun-Tzu's wisdom serves as a timeless source of inspiration, reminding us that the principles of self-awareness, adaptability, resilience, strategy, and leadership are the keys to maintaining the entrepreneurial flame.

In the pursuit of your business endeavors, remember that your passion and determination not only propel you forward but also inspire others to follow their dreams.

Your unwavering commitment to your vision has the power to ignite change, create impact, and leave a lasting legacy that extends far beyond your business.

Your journey is a testament to the indomitable spirit of human ambition, and it serves as a beacon of hope for those who dare to dream.

The Eternal Flame of Innovation

In the heart of every entrepreneur, there resides an eternal flame of innovation—a relentless desire to create, improve, and make a difference. This flame, fueled by passion and determination, has the power to transcend the ordinary and ignite extraordinary change.

As you navigate the challenges and triumphs of modern entrepreneurship, remember that it's not only about reaching the destination but also about savoring the journey.

Each obstacle overcome, each goal achieved, and each setback endured adds depth to your story, fueling the flames of your passion and determination.

The Ripple Effect

Your unwavering commitment to your entrepreneurial vision has a profound ripple effect. It inspires others around you—your team, your customers, and even future generations of entrepreneurs. Your passion becomes contagious, and your determination sets a precedent for what is possible.

In your moments of doubt or weariness, remember the impact you've already had and the lives you've touched.

Consider the aspiring entrepreneur who looks up to you as a role model or the customer whose life is positively transformed by your product or service.

These are the sparks ignited by your passion, and they continue to burn brightly.

A Legacy of Courage

In the annals of history, the names of great entrepreneurs are etched with stories of courage, tenacity, and audacity.

They dared to dream when others doubted, they pressed on when obstacles seemed insurmountable, and they redefined industries through their unwavering belief in their vision.

As a modern entrepreneur, you stand on the shoulders of these giants. You inherit a legacy of courage and a tradition of pushing the boundaries of what is possible.

Your journey is not merely about business; it is about contributing to the collective human spirit of innovation and progress.

Embracing the Journey

The flame of passion and determination is not a finite resource—it grows stronger with every challenge conquered. It thrives on resilience, adapts to change, and finds inspiration in the unlikeliest of places.

Embrace the journey with an open heart, knowing that each step forward, regardless of its size, keeps the flame burning.

In the spirit of Sun-Tzu's wisdom, understand that the path of entrepreneurship is not linear—it's a dynamic battlefield where victory lies not only in triumph but also in the unwavering resolve to keep moving forward.

Your passion and determination are your most formidable allies in this quest.

The Entrepreneurial Anthem

In closing, let the anthem of modern entrepreneurship be one of unyielding passion and undeterred determination. Let it echo through the corridors of innovation, inspiring dreamers to become doers, and challengers to become conquerors.

May your entrepreneurial flame burn bright, illuminating a path of endless possibilities. May your passion drive you to new heights, and your determination propel you through every trial.

And may your journey be a testament to the eternal fire that resides within the heart of every entrepreneur.

For as long as entrepreneurs like you continue to chase their dreams with unwavering fervor, the world will forever be a place of boundless innovation, progress, and limitless potential.

In this chapter, we've explored the enduring qualities of passion and determination that drive modern entrepreneurs, drawing inspiration from the wisdom of Sun-Tzu.

Chapter 13

The Endgame: Exit Strategies

In the grand strategy of modern entrepreneurship, the concept of an "exit strategy" may initially seem at odds with the timeless wisdom of Sun-Tzu's "Art of War."

After all, Sun-Tzu's teachings emphasize victory, not exit. However, as entrepreneurs, we must recognize that victory can take many forms, including knowing when to exit a venture gracefully and profitably.

This chapter delves into the crucial yet often overlooked aspect of entrepreneurship: exit strategies.

It explores how Sun-Tzu's principles of strategic planning, adaptation, and long-term vision can guide entrepreneurs in making well-informed decisions about the future of their ventures.

The Essence of Exit Strategies

An exit strategy is a predefined plan for how an entrepreneur or investor intends to exit their investment or business venture. It provides a roadmap for the entrepreneur to achieve specific financial or non-financial goals, whether it's selling the business, going public, merging with another company, or simply stepping back while maintaining ownership.

Why Exit Strategies Matter:

Exit strategies are not a sign of giving up; they are a sign of strategic foresight. Entrepreneurs who plan their exits carefully are better equipped to maximize returns, mitigate risks, and ensure the long-term sustainability of their businesses.

The Importance of Timing:

Just as Sun-Tzu emphasized the significance of timing in warfare, timing is critical in exit strategies. An exit executed at the right moment can yield substantial rewards, while delaying or exiting prematurely can have adverse consequences.

Aligning with Goals:

Exit strategies should align with the entrepreneur's personal and financial goals. Whether the aim is to achieve financial security, pursue new opportunities, or leave a lasting legacy, the exit strategy should serve as a means to those ends.

Sun-Tzu's Wisdom Applied

While Sun-Tzu's "Art of War" may not explicitly address exit strategies, its principles can be applied metaphorically to the entrepreneurial battlefield of exits:

1. Long-Term Vision:

Sun-Tzu encouraged leaders to maintain a long-term perspective. Entrepreneurs should approach exit strategies with a vision that extends beyond immediate gains, considering how the exit fits into their broader goals and legacy.

2. Strategic Planning:

Just as Sun-Tzu emphasized the importance of strategy, entrepreneurs must strategically plan their exits. This involves assessing market conditions, valuing the business, and identifying potential buyers or partners.

3. Adaptability:

Sun-Tzu's teachings on adaptability resonate with exit strategies. Entrepreneurs must remain flexible and ready to adjust their exit plans in response to changing market dynamics or unexpected opportunities.

4. Risk Mitigation:

Sun-Tzu advised minimizing risks whenever possible. In exit strategies, entrepreneurs should aim to minimize potential obstacles or uncertainties that could hinder a smooth exit process.

5. Timing:

Timing was a critical element in Sun-Tzu's strategy. Entrepreneurs should carefully consider the timing of their exit to maximize returns and align with market conditions.

Types of Exit Strategies

Entrepreneurs have several exit options at their disposal. Here are some common exit strategies:

1.   IPO (Initial Public Offering):

Taking a company public through an IPO involves selling shares to the public via a stock exchange. This exit strategy can provide access to significant capital and liquidity for early investors.

2. Acquisition:

Selling the business to a larger company is a common exit strategy. Acquisitions can offer entrepreneurs financial rewards, resources, and opportunities for growth.

3. Merger:

Merging with another company of similar size can create synergies and lead to mutual benefits. Entrepreneurs may choose this exit strategy to strengthen their market position.

4. Management Buyout (MBO):

In an MBO, the existing management team or employees purchase the company from the entrepreneur. This allows for continuity while providing an exit for the owner.

5. Strategic Partnering:

Partnering with a strategic investor or company can offer access to resources and distribution channels while allowing the entrepreneur to retain some level of control.

6. Liquidation:

In some cases, liquidation may be the only viable exit option. This involves selling off the company's assets and closing the business.

The Exit Strategy Journey

The decision to execute an exit strategy should not be impulsive but rather the culmination of a well-considered journey:

1.   Define Clear Goals:

Begin by defining your personal and financial goals for the exit. What do you hope to achieve, and what legacy do you want to leave?

2. Strategic Planning:

Conduct a thorough analysis of your business, market conditions, and potential exit options. Seek professional advice if necessary.

3. Timing and Market Conditions:

Assess the current state of the market and evaluate whether it's favorable for your chosen exit strategy. Timing is crucial for maximizing returns.

4. Execution:

Execute the exit strategy meticulously, ensuring that all legal, financial, and operational aspects are in order. Communication with stakeholders is vital.

5. Post-Exit Plans:

Consider what you'll do after the exit. Whether it's embarking on a new venture, enjoying retirement, or pursuing philanthropic endeavors, have a plan in place.

6. Legacy and Impact:

Reflect on the legacy you want to leave through your exit. How will your business and its impact endure beyond your ownership?

The Emotional Aspect of Exiting

Exiting a business can be an emotional journey. Entrepreneurs often have a deep attachment to their ventures, having poured their passion, time, and energy into them.

It's essential to acknowledge and manage the emotional aspects of exit strategies:

1. Embrace Change:

Recognize that exit is a natural part of the entrepreneurial journey. Embrace the change as an opportunity for growth and new beginnings.

2. Celebrate Achievements:

Take time to celebrate your achievements and the impact your business has had. Share these moments with your team and stakeholders to create a sense of closure and accomplishment.

3. Seek Support:

Reach out to mentors, friends, and fellow entrepreneurs who have gone through similar exits. Their insights and emotional support can be invaluable.

4. Reflect and Reconnect:

Use the exit as an opportunity to reflect on your journey and reconnect with your passions and personal goals. What new adventures await you?

5. Stay Engaged:

Consider staying involved in the entrepreneurial community through mentoring, investing, or advisory roles. Your experience can continue to make a difference.

6. Legacy and Impact:

Focus on the legacy you leave behind. How will your business continue to impact the lives of customers, employees, and the community?

A Timeless Transition

In the grand tapestry of entrepreneurship, exit strategies are not merely the end of one chapter; they are the beginning of another. They represent the transition from one venture to the next, from one set of aspirations to another.

Sun-Tzu's wisdom reminds us that every strategic decision we make, including our exit strategies, should be guided by a clear vision, adaptability to changing circumstances, and an unwavering commitment to our long-term goals.

As modern entrepreneurs, we stand on the shoulders of those who have come before us, and we bear the responsibility of shaping the future.

Our exit strategies are not just about personal gain; they are about the continuity of our vision, the well-being of our teams, and the lasting impact on the world.

In your entrepreneurial journey, remember that an exit is not a sign of surrender; it's a declaration of victory—a victory that allows you to transition to new horizons while ensuring the legacy of your accomplishments endures.

May your exit strategies be guided by wisdom, driven by purpose, and executed with grace. And may each exit be the precursor to a new chapter of innovation, growth, and enduring impact.

In the final pages of your entrepreneurial story, the emotional tone takes center stage. Exiting a venture is not just a financial transaction; it's a profound moment in your life's narrative. It's where the passion and determination that fueled your journey culminate in a new chapter of your life.

The Bittersweet Farewell

As you stand at the threshold of your exit, you may experience a whirlwind of emotions. There's the excitement of what lies ahead, the satisfaction of achieving your goals, and the anticipation of a well-deserved rest.

But intertwined with these positive emotions, there can also be a sense of loss.

Your business, like a trusted companion, has been with you through the ups and downs.

It's seen your vision come to life, witnessed your triumphs, and stood beside you during the challenging moments.

Letting go can feel like bidding farewell to an old friend.
It's okay to mourn this parting.

Acknowledge the emotional complexity of the moment. Share your feelings with your team and loved ones. Celebrate the memories and lessons learned along the way.

The bittersweet farewell is a testament to the profound impact your venture has had on your life.

The Spark of New Beginnings

While one chapter ends, another begins. Your exit strategy is not just about closing a door; it's about opening new ones. As you embark on this fresh journey, let your heart be open to the possibilities that await.

Consider the impact you can make beyond your business. Whether it's mentoring aspiring entrepreneurs, pursuing philanthropic endeavors, or simply enjoying a well-deserved break, there's a world of opportunities ahead.

Embrace these with the same passion and determination that guided your entrepreneurial path.

Leaving a Lasting Legacy

Entrepreneurs are more than just business owners; they are architects of change. Your legacy is not solely measured by the financial success of your venture but by the enduring impact you leave behind.

How has your business transformed lives, enriched communities, or advanced industries?

Take a moment to reflect on the legacy you've built. Whether it's in the form of innovations, employment opportunities, or contributions to a cause you care about, your legacy lives on.

Consider how you can continue to nurture and amplify this impact in your post-exit journey.

A Community of Entrepreneurs

Entrepreneurship is a vibrant and interconnected community. As you exit one venture, you become part of a network of experienced entrepreneurs who have navigated similar transitions. Share your insights, offer guidance, and become a mentor to the next generation of innovators.

Your experiences, both the successes and the challenges, are invaluable lessons that can empower others on their own entrepreneurial journeys. Your wisdom can light the way for those who follow in your footsteps.

The Eternal Entrepreneurial Spirit

The entrepreneurial spirit that ignited your journey does not diminish with an exit; it continues to burn brightly within you. It's the relentless desire to create, innovate, and make a difference in the world.

This spirit is not bound by the confines of a single venture; it's a force that transcends and persists.

As you exit, remember that you carry this eternal entrepreneurial spirit with you. It's the fire that drove you to embark on your entrepreneurial journey in the first place, and it's the flame that will continue to guide your path forward.

Conclusion: The Next Chapter

In the story of modern entrepreneurship, an exit is not the end; it's a pivotal plot twist. It's where the culmination of your hard work and dedication takes shape, and where the legacy of your impact begins to unfold.

Embrace this moment with grace, acknowledging the emotional depth it holds. Cherish the memories, celebrate your achievements, and prepare for the exciting journey that awaits. Your exit is not just a chapter's end; it's the prologue to the next chapter of your life's extraordinary narrative.

May your exit be a testament to the passion, determination, and resilience that define modern entrepreneurs. And may your future endeavors be infused with the same unwavering spirit that has carried you this far.

In this chapter, we've explored the emotional depth of exit strategies in modern entrepreneurship, recognizing that an exit is not just a business decision but a profound life transition.

Chapter 14

Beyond Sun-Tzu: Continuous Learning and Adaptation

In the pages of "Sun-Tzu's Art of War Strategies for Modern Entrepreneurs," we've journeyed through the ancient wisdom of Sun-Tzu's teachings, discovering timeless principles that have guided warriors and, in our context, entrepreneurs for centuries.

Yet, in the ever-evolving landscape of modern entrepreneurship, we find that the wisdom of the past, while invaluable, is only the beginning of our quest for success.

This chapter is a celebration of learning, adaptation, and the recognition that our entrepreneurial journey is an ongoing evolution.

As we look beyond Sun-Tzu's sage counsel, we find that our ability to adapt, grow, and learn continuously is the ultimate strategy for thriving in the dynamic world of business.

The Unceasing Pursuit of Knowledge

Sun-Tzu's teachings emphasized the importance of understanding oneself and one's adversaries. In our world, this translates to understanding our market, competition, and, most crucially, ourselves. Continuous learning is the key that unlocks this understanding.

1. Embrace Curiosity:

Cultivate an insatiable curiosity about your industry, market trends, emerging technologies, and consumer behavior. Be a perpetual student of your craft.

2. Stay Informed:

The business landscape is constantly shifting. Stay informed through industry publications, news, and thought leaders. Knowledge is your compass in uncharted territories.

3. Seek Mentorship:

The wisdom of experienced mentors is an invaluable asset. Seek guidance from those who have walked the path before you, and never underestimate the power of a trusted advisor.

4. Continual Improvement:

Just as you strive to improve your business processes, focus on self-improvement. Identify your strengths and weaknesses and commit to personal growth.

5. Learn from Failure:

Failure is a relentless teacher. Embrace it, dissect it, and derive lessons from it. Every setback is an opportunity for growth.

The Art of Adaptation

In Sun-Tzu's world, adaptability was a cornerstone of victory. The ability to pivot, adjust strategies, and respond to changing circumstances was paramount. In the world of modern entrepreneurship, adaptability remains the linchpin of success.

1. Agility in Business:

Build an agile organization that can swiftly respond to market shifts. This includes flexible business models, nimble teams, and the ability to pivot when necessary.

2. Market Sensing:

Develop a keen sense of market trends and consumer preferences. The ability to anticipate change and adapt your offerings accordingly is a competitive advantage.

3. Embrace Technology:

Technology is a catalyst for change. Embrace digital transformation and harness the power of technology to enhance your business operations and offerings.

4. Customer-Centric Approach:

Put your customers at the center of your business. Continuously gather feedback and adapt your products and services to meet their evolving needs.

5. Experimentation and Innovation:

Encourage a culture of experimentation and innovation within your organization. This fosters an environment where adaptation thrives.

The Entrepreneurial Growth Mindset

In the spirit of continuous learning and adaptation, it's essential to cultivate a growth mindset. This mindset, popularized by psychologist Carol Dweck, is the belief that abilities and intelligence can be developed through dedication and hard work.

1. Embrace Challenges:

Challenges are opportunities for growth. Rather than avoiding them, confront them head-on, knowing that each challenge is a chance to learn and adapt.

2. Learn from Criticism:

Criticism, like feedback, is a valuable source of learning. Welcome constructive criticism as a means to improve and grow.

3. Persistence and Resilience:

Understand that setbacks are temporary. A growth mindset fuels persistence and resilience, enabling you to bounce back from failures.

4. Embrace Change:

Change is the only constant in the business world. Embrace it as an opportunity to learn, adapt, and evolve.

The Entrepreneurial Renaissance

In the world of modern entrepreneurship, there is a renaissance of learning and adaptation—an era where the quest for knowledge is unending, and the ability to adapt is a superpower.

Entrepreneurs today are not just business leaders; they are perpetual students, eternal optimists, and relentless innovators.

This renaissance is characterized by the belief that there are no limits to what can be achieved through continuous learning and adaptation.

It's a recognition that the journey of entrepreneurship is not a linear path but a dynamic, ever-evolving quest for excellence.

Conclusion: Beyond Mastery

As we conclude our exploration of Sun-Tzu's wisdom and venture beyond, remember that the pursuit of knowledge and the art of adaptation are not separate from his teachings; they are the essence of mastery.

In the realm of modern entrepreneurship, we stand on the shoulders of ancient wisdom, fortified by the knowledge that our journey is one of perpetual growth and transformation.

Our battles are not against adversaries but against complacency, our victories not just in market share but in the relentless pursuit of excellence.

May your entrepreneurial journey be a testament to the enduring power of continuous learning and adaptation.

As you navigate the ever-changing landscape of business, may you find joy in the quest for knowledge and resilience in the face of change.

In your journey beyond Sun-Tzu, may you discover that the greatest strategy of all is the unceasing commitment to become better, adapt faster, and, in doing so, make a lasting impact on the world.

In the emotional heart of our entrepreneurial journey lies the recognition that growth and adaptation are not just strategies for success; they are deeply personal and transformative experiences.

It's about more than just achieving business objectives; it's about evolving as individuals and contributing to the greater good.

The Joy of Discovery

Imagine the joy of discovering a new insight that transforms your approach to business. It's the moment you read a groundbreaking book, attend an inspiring conference, or engage in a thought-provoking conversation that leaves you brimming with new ideas.

Embrace these moments of discovery with childlike wonder. They are the sparks that ignite innovation, invigorate your spirit, and remind you that the journey of learning is a thrilling adventure.

The Humility of Adaptation

In the pursuit of knowledge and adaptation, humility is a constant companion. It's the acknowledgment that there is always more to learn, and no matter how successful you become, there are new horizons to explore.

Embrace humility as a source of strength. It allows you to seek guidance, learn from others, and pivot when necessary. It's a reminder that the most profound growth often comes from moments of vulnerability.

The Resilience of the Human Spirit

Our entrepreneurial journey is a testament to the resilience of the human spirit. It's the ability to face adversity, adapt to change, and emerge stronger than before. Every setback is a chapter in the story of your resilience.

Embrace the challenges and setbacks as opportunities to build resilience. They are not roadblocks but stepping stones on your path to greatness. The ability to rise above challenges is a testament to your character and determination.

The Legacy of Impact

As modern entrepreneurs, we have the privilege of creating impact not only through our businesses but also through our commitment to learning and adaptation. The legacy we leave extends beyond balance sheets and profit margins; it encompasses the lives we touch and the positive change we inspire.

Embrace the responsibility of your legacy with a sense of purpose. Consider how your journey of continuous learning and adaptation can inspire others to pursue their dreams, contribute to society, and make the world a better place.

The Uncharted Territories

In the world of modern entrepreneurship, we are explorers of uncharted territories. It's a thrilling journey where the map is constantly redrawn, and the destination is ever-shifting. The unknown is not a source of fear but a canvas for innovation.

Embrace the uncertainty as an opportunity for creativity. It's in the uncharted territories that groundbreaking ideas are born, and new paths to success are forged. The willingness to venture into the unknown is the hallmark of a true entrepreneur.

The Journey Continues

As we conclude this chapter and look beyond Sun-Tzu's teachings, remember that the entrepreneurial journey is a magnificent tapestry of emotions, experiences, and discoveries. It's a journey that transcends business and touches the essence of what it means to be human.

Embrace every moment with gratitude and an open heart. Celebrate your successes, learn from your failures, and continue to adapt and grow. Your journey is an inspiration to others, a source of personal fulfillment, and a testament to the enduring spirit of entrepreneurship.

May your pursuit of knowledge be boundless, your capacity for adaptation unyielding, and your legacy of impact everlasting. As you navigate the emotional landscape of your entrepreneurial journey, may you find profound joy, resilience, and purpose in every step.

In this chapter, we've delved into the emotional depth of continuous learning and adaptation in modern entrepreneurship, recognizing that our journey is not just a quest for success but a profound exploration of the human spirit.

100 aphorism and phrases of 'Sun-Tzu's Art of War'

"In the chaos of battle, find your inner calm."

"To win without fighting is the greatest victory of all."

"Adapt or be broken by the winds of change."

"Strike when your enemy least expects it."

"The path to victory is paved with patience."

"A cunning strategy can turn the tide of fate."

"Know your enemy as you know yourself."

"The greatest warriors are masters of deception."

"In unity, strength; in division, weakness."

"Opportunities multiply as they are seized."

"Defend what is yours with unwavering determination."

"A leader's clarity guides the way for the army."

"The best offense is a flawless defense."

"Conquer your doubts before you conquer your foes."

"Tread lightly, but carry a heavy resolve."

"In the heat of battle, silence can be the deadliest weapon."

"The art of war is the art of survival."

"Seize the moment, for it may not come again."

"A wise general values the counsel of advisors."

"Victory belongs to those who dare to dream."

"A well-prepared army fears no enemy."

"Appear weak when you are strong; appear strong when you are weak."

"The sun sets on those who hesitate."

"Inaction is the ally of defeat."

"The warrior who rushes blindly into battle invites disaster."

"Patience can turn a foe into a friend."

"The key to victory lies in the element of surprise."

"A well-fed army marches with strength and purpose."

"The path of honor is paved with sacrifice."

"The shadow of doubt can eclipse even the brightest strategy."

"A leader who listens learns."

"Strength flows from the heart, not just the muscles."

"The wise general wins battles without shedding blood."

"A warrior's strength lies in adaptability."

"The true battle is often fought within one's own mind."

"Strike swiftly and decisively when the opportunity arises."

"A leader who inspires loyalty is unstoppable."

"A hasty retreat can lead to ultimate victory."

"The art of war is as much about diplomacy as it is about combat."

"Victory is born from the ashes of adversity."

"The battlefield reveals the true character of a leader."

"An army united in purpose is invincible."

"The strongest fortress is a patient heart."

"The wisest general avoids unnecessary conflicts."

"The path to success is often hidden in plain sight."

"A well-fed mind is as crucial as a well-fed body."

"Distract and conquer, for the mind is a powerful weapon."

"A leader's strength is measured by the loyalty of their followers."

"In the face of danger, courage shines brightest."

"The strategist sees the invisible and achieves the impossible."

"A leader who values the lives of their soldiers is revered."

"Victory is sweetest when it's shared with allies."

"The greatest battles are often fought silently."

"A leader's words can inspire or destroy."

"An army's morale is the foundation of its strength."

"The path of least resistance often leads to defeat."

"Success is the offspring of preparation and opportunity."

"A leader who leads by example commands the greatest respect."

"The fog of war can obscure even the clearest vision."

"A wise leader understands the value of retreat."

"The river of time flows, and so must your strategy."

"Courage is the armor that shields the heart."

"In the midst of chaos, find your center."

"The greatest victories are won without a drop of blood."

"The seeds of victory are sown in the soil of strategy."

"A leader's integrity is their most powerful weapon."

"To conquer others, conquer yourself first."

"A warrior's spirit shines brightest in the darkest hours."

"Unity is the cornerstone of any great achievement."

"A leader who knows when to yield can endure."

"The art of war is a dance of strategy and timing."

"A swift withdrawal can be a strategic advance."

"A leader's vision lights the path to victory."

"The battlefield is a canvas for the art of strategy."

"In adversity, find strength; in strength, find victory."

"A wise leader values every soldier's contribution."

"To conquer fear is to conquer one's greatest enemy."

"In the face of overwhelming odds, stand firm."

"A leader's legacy lives on in the hearts of their followers."

"The greatest generals win battles before they begin."

"The winds of change can carry you to new heights."

"To master others is a sign of strength; to master yourself is true power."

"A leader's humility can disarm the proudest foe."

"Fortify your mind, and your resolve will be unbreakable."

"To know when to fight and when to yield is the essence of wisdom."

"The path of victory is often paved with sacrifice."

"A leader who values the welfare of their troops will be revered."

"In chaos, find opportunity."

"The greatest generals are masters of timing."

"A wise leader knows when to be silent."

"Victory is the sweetest reward for the vigilant."

"The strategist turns obstacles into stepping stones."

"A leader's strength is their ability to adapt to any situation."

"The calmest waters can hide the strongest currents."

"To win the war, win the hearts of your soldiers."

"A leader's legacy lives on in the lessons they impart."

"The strongest fortress is a united front."

"A leader's wisdom is a beacon in the darkest night."

"In the face of adversity, rise like the sun."

"The art of war is the art of life itself."

These aphorisms and phrases capture the essence of Sun Tzu's "Art of War" and emphasize the importance of strategy, leadership, and inner strength in both warfare and life.

THE ART OF WAR
BY SUN-TZU

Complete Original Text

Translated by Lionel Giles

(Originally published 1910)

CHAPTER 1.

LAYING PLANS

1. Sun Tzu said: The art of war is of vital importance to the State.

2. It is a matter of life and death, a road either to safety or to ruin. Hence it is a subject of inquiry which can on no account be neglected.

3. The art of war, then, is governed by five constant factors, to be taken into account in one's deliberations, when seeking to determine the conditions obtaining in the field.

4. These are: (1) The Moral Law; (2) Heaven; (3) Earth; (4) The Commander; (5) Method and discipline.

5. The MORAL LAW causes the people to be in complete accord with their ruler, so that they will follow him regardless of their lives, undismayed by any danger.

6. HEAVEN signifies night and day, cold and heat, times and seasons.

7. EARTH comprises distances, great and small; danger and security; open ground and narrow passes; the chances of life and death.

8. The COMMANDER stands for the virtues of wisdom, sincerity, benevolence, courage and strictness.

9. By METHOD AND DISCIPLINE are to be understood the marshaling of the army in its proper subdivisions, the graduations of rank among the officers, the maintenance of roads by which supplies may reach the army, and the control of military expenditure.

10. These five heads should be familiar to every general: he who knows them will be victorious; he who knows them not will fail.

11. Therefore, in your deliberations, when seeking to determine the military conditions, let them be made the basis of a comparison, in this wise:

12. (1) Which of the two sovereigns is imbued with the Moral law? (2) Which of the two generals has most ability? (3) With whom lie the advantages derived from Heaven and Earth? (4) On which side is discipline most rigorously enforced? (5) Which army is stronger? (6) On which side are officers and men more highly trained? (7) In which army is there the greater constancy both in reward and punishment?

13. By means of these seven considerations I can forecast victory or defeat.

14. The general that hearkens to my counsel and acts upon it, will conquer: let such a one be retained in command! The general that

hearkens not to my counsel nor acts upon it, will suffer defeat: let such a one be dismissed!

15. While heeding the profit of my counsel, avail yourself also of any helpful circumstances over and beyond the ordinary rules.

16. According as circumstances are favorable, one should modify one's plans.

17. All warfare is based on deception.

18. Hence, when able to attack, we must seem unable; when using our forces, we must seem inactive; when we are near, we must make the enemy believe we are far away; when far away, we must make him believe we are near.

19. Hold out baits to entice the enemy. Feign disorder, and crush him.

20. If he is secure at all points, be prepared for him. If he is in superior strength, evade him.

21. If your opponent is of choleric temper, seek to irritate him. Pretend to be weak, that he may grow arrogant.

22. If he is taking his ease, give him no rest. If his forces are united, separate them.

23. Attack him where he is unprepared, appear where you are not expected.

24. These military devices, leading to victory, must not be divulged beforehand.

25. Now the general who wins a battle makes many calculations in his temple ere the battle is fought. The general who loses a battle makes but few calculations beforehand.

Thus do many calculations lead to victory, and few calculations to defeat: how much more no calculation at all! It is by attention to this point that I can foresee who is likely to win or lose.

CHAPTER 2.

WAGING WAR

1. Sun Tzu said: In the operations of war, where there are in the field a thousand swift chariots, as many heavy chariots, and a hundred thousand mail-clad soldiers, with provisions enough to carry them a thousand LI, the expenditure at home and at the front, including entertainment of guests, small items such as glue and paint, and sums spent on chariots and armor, will reach the total of a thousand ounces of silver per day. Such is the cost of raising an army of 100,000 men.

2. When you engage in actual fighting, if victory is long in coming, then men's weapons will grow dull and their ardor will be damped. If you lay siege to a town, you will exhaust your strength.

3. Again, if the campaign is protracted, the resources of the State will not be equal to the strain.

4. Now, when your weapons are dulled, your ardor damped, your strength exhausted and your treasure spent, other chieftains will spring up to take advantage of your extremity. Then no man, however wise, will be able to avert the consequences that must ensue.

5. Thus, though we have heard of stupid haste in war, cleverness has never been seen associated with long delays.

6. There is no instance of a country having benefited from prolonged warfare.

7. It is only one who is thoroughly acquainted with the evils of war that can thoroughly

understand the profitable way of carrying it on.

8. The skillful soldier does not raise a second levy, neither are his supply-wagons loaded more than twice.

9. Bring war material with you from home, but forage on the enemy. Thus the army will have food enough for its needs.

10. Poverty of the State exchequer causes an army to be maintained by contributions from a distance. Contributing to maintain an army at a distance causes the people to be impoverished.

11. On the other hand, the proximity of an army causes prices to go up; and high prices cause the people's substance to be drained away.

12. When their substance is drained away, the peasantry will be afflicted by heavy exactions.

13,14. With this loss of substance and exhaustion of strength, the homes of the people will be stripped bare, and three-tenths of their income will be dissipated; while government expenses for broken chariots, worn-out horses, breast-plates and helmets, bows and arrows, spears and shields, protective mantles, draught-oxen and heavy wagons, will amount to four-tenths of its total revenue.

15. Hence a wise general makes a point of foraging on the enemy. One cartload of the enemy's provisions is equivalent to twenty of one's own, and likewise a single PICUL of his provender is equivalent to twenty from one's own store.

16. Now in order to kill the enemy, our men must be roused to anger; that there may be advantage from defeating the enemy, they must have their rewards.

17. Therefore in chariot fighting, when ten or more chariots have been taken, those should be rewarded who took the first. Our own flags should be substituted for those of the enemy, and the chariots mingled and used in

conjunction with ours. The captured soldiers should be kindly treated and kept.

18. This is called, using the conquered foe to augment one's own strength.

19. In war, then, let your great object be victory, not lengthy campaigns.

20. Thus it may be known that the leader of armies is the arbiter of the people's fate, the man on whom it depends whether the nation shall be in peace or in peril.

CHAPTER 3.

ATTACK BY STRATAGEM

1. Sun Tzu said: In the practical art of war, the best thing of all is to take the enemy's country whole and intact; to shatter and destroy it is not so good. So, too, it is better to recapture an army entire than to destroy it, to capture a regiment, a detachment or a company entire than to destroy them.

2. Hence to fight and conquer in all your battles is not supreme excellence; supreme excellence consists in breaking the enemy's resistance without fighting.

3. Thus the highest form of generalship is to balk the enemy's plans; the next best is to prevent the junction of the enemy's forces; the next in order is to attack the enemy's army in the field; and the worst policy of all is to besiege walled cities.

4. The rule is, not to besiege walled cities if it can possibly be avoided. The preparation of mantlets, movable shelters, and various implements of war, will take up three whole months; and the piling up of mounds over against the walls will take three months more.

5. The general, unable to control his irritation, will launch his men to the assault like swarming ants, with the result that one-third of his men are slain, while the town still remains untaken. Such are the disastrous effects of a siege.

6. Therefore the skillful leader subdues the enemy's troops without any fighting; he captures their cities without laying siege to them; he overthrows their kingdom without lengthy operations in the field.

7. With his forces intact he will dispute the mastery of the Empire, and thus, without losing a man, his triumph will be complete. This is the method of attacking by stratagem.

8. It is the rule in war, if our forces are ten to the enemy's one, to surround him; if five to one, to attack him; if twice as numerous, to divide our army into two.

9. If equally matched, we can offer battle; if slightly inferior in numbers, we can avoid the enemy; if quite unequal in every way, we can flee from him.

10. Hence, though an obstinate fight may be made by a small force, in the end it must be captured by the larger force.

11. Now the general is the bulwark of the State; if the bulwark is complete at all points; the State will be strong; if the bulwark is defective, the State will be weak.

12. There are three ways in which a ruler can bring misfortune upon his army:

13. (1) By commanding the army to advance or to retreat, being ignorant of the fact that it cannot obey. This is called hobbling the army.

14. (2) By attempting to govern an army in the same way as he administers a kingdom, being ignorant of the conditions which obtain in an army. This causes restlessness in the soldier's minds.

15. (3) By employing the officers of his army without discrimination, through ignorance of the military principle of adaptation to circumstances. This shakes the confidence of the soldiers.

16. But when the army is restless and distrustful, trouble is sure to come from the other feudal princes. This is simply bringing anarchy into the army, and flinging victory away.

17. Thus we may know that there are five essentials for victory: (1) He will win who knows when to fight and when not to fight. (2) He will win who knows how to handle both superior and inferior forces. (3) He will

win whose army is animated by the same spirit throughout all its ranks. (4) He will win who, prepared himself, waits to take the enemy unprepared. (5) He will win who has military capacity and is not interfered with by the sovereign.

18. Hence the saying: If you know the enemy and know yourself, you need not fear the result of a hundred battles. If you know yourself but not the enemy, for every victory gained you will also suffer a defeat. If you know neither the enemy nor yourself, you will succumb in every battle.

CHAPTER 4.

TACTICAL DISPOSITIONS

1. Sun Tzu said: The good fighters of old first put themselves beyond the possibility of defeat, and then waited for an opportunity of defeating the enemy.

2. To secure ourselves against defeat lies in our own hands, but the opportunity of defeating the enemy is provided by the enemy himself.

3. Thus the good fighter is able to secure himself against defeat, but cannot make certain of defeating the enemy.

4. Hence the saying: One may KNOW how to conquer without being able to DO it.

5. Security against defeat implies defensive tactics; ability to defeat the enemy means taking the offensive.

6. Standing on the defensive indicates insufficient strength; attacking, a superabundance of strength.

7. The general who is skilled in defense hides in the most secret recesses of the earth; he who is skilled in attack flashes forth from the topmost heights of heaven. Thus on the one hand we have ability to protect ourselves; on the other, a victory that is complete.

8. To see victory only when it is within the ken of the common herd is not the acme of excellence.

9. Neither is it the acme of excellence if you fight and conquer and the whole Empire says, "Well done!"

10. To lift an autumn hair is no sign of great strength; to see the sun and moon is no sign of sharp sight; to hear the noise of thunder is no sign of a quick ear.

11. What the ancients called a clever fighter is one who not only wins, but excels in winning with ease.

12. Hence his victories bring him neither reputation for wisdom nor credit for courage.

13. He wins his battles by making no mistakes. Making no mistakes is what establishes the certainty of victory, for it means conquering an enemy that is already defeated.

14. Hence the skillful fighter puts himself into a position which makes defeat impossible, and does not miss the moment for defeating the enemy.

15. Thus it is that in war the victorious strategist only seeks battle after the victory has been won, whereas he who is destined to defeat first fights and afterwards looks for victory.

16. The consummate leader cultivates the moral law, and strictly adheres to method and discipline; thus it is in his power to control success.

17. In respect of military method, we have, firstly, Measurement; secondly, Estimation of quantity; thirdly, Calculation; fourthly, Balancing of chances; fifthly, Victory.

18. Measurement owes its existence to Earth; Estimation of quantity to Measurement; Calculation to Estimation of quantity; Balancing of chances to Calculation; and Victory to Balancing of chances.

19. A victorious army opposed to a routed one, is as a pound's weight placed in the scale against a single grain.

20. The onrush of a conquering force is like the bursting of pent-up waters into a chasm a thousand fathoms deep.

CHAPTER 5.

ENERGY

1. Sun Tzu said: The control of a large force is the same principle as the control of a few men: it is merely a question of dividing up their numbers.

2. Fighting with a large army under your command is nowise different from fighting with a small one: it is merely a question of instituting signs and signals.

3. To ensure that your whole host may withstand the brunt of the enemy's attack and remain unshaken---this is effected by maneuvers direct and indirect.

4. That the impact of your army may be like a grindstone dashed against an egg---this is effected by the science of weak points and strong.

5. In all fighting, the direct method may be used for joining battle, but indirect methods will be needed in order to secure victory.

6. Indirect tactics, efficiently applied, are inexhaustible as Heaven and Earth, unending as the flow of rivers and streams; like the sun and moon, they end but to begin anew; like the four seasons, they pass away to return once more.

7. There are not more than five musical notes, yet the combinations of these five give rise to more melodies than can ever be heard.

8. There are not more than five primary colors (blue, yellow, red, white, and black), yet in combination they produce more hues than can ever been seen.

9. There are not more than five cardinal tastes (sour, acrid, salt, sweet, bitter), yet

combinations of them yield more flavors than can ever be tasted.

10. In battle, there are not more than two methods of attack: the direct and the indirect; yet these two in combination give rise to an endless series of maneuvers.

11. The direct and the indirect lead on to each other in turn. It is like moving in a circle---you never come to an end. Who can exhaust the possibilities of their combination?

12. The onset of troops is like the rush of a torrent which will even roll stones along in its course.

13. The quality of decision is like the well-timed swoop of a falcon which enables it to strike and destroy its victim.

14. Therefore the good fighter will be terrible in his onset, and prompt in his decision.

15. Energy may be likened to the bending of a crossbow; decision, to the releasing of a trigger.

16. Amid the turmoil and tumult of battle, there may be seeming disorder and yet no real disorder at all; amid confusion and chaos, your array may be without head or tail, yet it will be proof against defeat.

17. Simulated disorder postulates perfect discipline, simulated fear postulates courage; simulated weakness postulates strength.

18. Hiding order beneath the cloak of disorder is simply a question of subdivision; concealing courage under a show of timidity presupposes a fund of latent energy; masking strength with weakness is to be effected by tactical dispositions.

19. Thus one who is skillful at keeping the enemy on the move maintains deceitful appearances, according to which the enemy will act. He sacrifices something, that the enemy may snatch at it.

20. By holding out baits, he keeps him on the march; then with a body of picked men he lies in wait for him.

21. The clever combatant looks to the effect of combined energy, and does not require too much from individuals. Hence his ability to pick out the right men and utilize combined energy.

22. When he utilizes combined energy, his fighting men become as it were like unto rolling logs or stones. For it is the nature of a log or stone to remain motionless on level ground, and to move when on a slope; if four-cornered, to come to a standstill, but if round-shaped, to go rolling down.

23. Thus the energy developed by good fighting men is as the momentum of a round stone rolled down a mountain thousands of feet in height. So much on the subject of energy.

CHAPTER 6.

WEAK POINTS AND STRONG

1. Sun Tzu said: Whoever is first in the field and awaits the coming of the enemy, will be fresh for the fight; whoever is second in the field and has to hasten to battle will arrive exhausted.

2. Therefore the clever combatant imposes his will on the enemy, but does not allow the enemy's will to be imposed on him.

3. By holding out advantages to him, he can cause the enemy to approach of his own accord; or, by inflicting damage, he can make it impossible for the enemy to draw near.

4. If the enemy is taking his ease, he can harass him; if well supplied with food, he can starve him out; if quietly encamped, he can force him to move.

5. Appear at points which the enemy must hasten to defend; march swiftly to places where you are not expected.

6. An army may march great distances without distress, if it marches through country where the enemy is not.

7. You can be sure of succeeding in your attacks if you only attack places which are undefended. You can ensure the safety of your defense if you only hold positions that cannot be attacked.

8. Hence that general is skillful in attack whose opponent does not know what to defend; and he is skillful in defense whose opponent does not know what to attack.

9. O divine art of subtlety and secrecy! Through you we learn to be invisible, through

you inaudible; and hence we can hold the enemy's fate in our hands.

10. You may advance and be absolutely irresistible, if you make for the enemy's weak points; you may retire and be safe from pursuit if your movements are more rapid than those of the enemy.

11. If we wish to fight, the enemy can be forced to an engagement even though he be sheltered behind a high rampart and a deep ditch. All we need do is attack some other place that he will be obliged to relieve.

12. If we do not wish to fight, we can prevent the enemy from engaging us even though the lines of our encampment be merely traced out on the ground. All we need do is to throw something odd and unaccountable in his way.

13. By discovering the enemy's dispositions and remaining invisible ourselves, we can keep our forces concentrated, while the enemy's must be divided.

14. We can form a single united body, while the enemy must split up into fractions. Hence there will be a whole pitted against separate parts of a whole, which means that we shall be many to the enemy's few.

15. And if we are able thus to attack an inferior force with a superior one, our opponents will be in dire straits.

16. The spot where we intend to fight must not be made known; for then the enemy will have to prepare against a possible attack at several different points; and his forces being thus distributed in many directions, the numbers we shall have to face at any given point will be proportionately few.

17. For should the enemy strengthen his van, he will weaken his rear; should he strengthen his rear, he will weaken his van; should he strengthen his left, he will weaken his right; should he strengthen his right, he will weaken his left. If he sends reinforcements everywhere, he will everywhere be weak.

18. Numerical weakness comes from having to prepare against possible attacks; numerical strength, from compelling our adversary to make these preparations against us.

19. Knowing the place and the time of the coming battle, we may concentrate from the greatest distances in order to fight.

20. But if neither time nor place be known, then the left wing will be impotent to succor the right, the right equally impotent to succor the left, the van unable to relieve the rear, or the rear to support the van. How much more so if the furthest portions of the army are anything under a hundred LI apart, and even the nearest are separated by several LI!

21. Though according to my estimate the soldiers of Yueh exceed our own in number, that shall advantage them nothing in the matter of victory. I say then that victory can be achieved.

22. Though the enemy be stronger in numbers, we may prevent him from fighting.

Scheme so as to discover his plans and the likelihood of their success.

23. Rouse him, and learn the principle of his activity or inactivity. Force him to reveal himself, so as to find out his vulnerable spots.

24. Carefully compare the opposing army with your own, so that you may know where strength is superabundant and where it is deficient.

25. In making tactical dispositions, the highest pitch you can attain is to conceal them; conceal your dispositions, and you will be safe from the prying of the subtlest spies, from the machinations of the wisest brains.

26. How victory may be produced for them out of the enemy's own tactics---that is what the multitude cannot comprehend.

27. All men can see the tactics whereby I conquer, but what none can see is the strategy out of which victory is evolved.

28. Do not repeat the tactics which have gained you one victory, but let your methods be regulated by the infinite variety of circumstances.

29. Military tactics are like unto water; for water in its natural course runs away from high places and hastens downwards.

30. So in war, the way is to avoid what is strong and to strike at what is weak.

31. Water shapes its course according to the nature of the ground over which it flows; the soldier works out his victory in relation to the foe whom he is facing.

32. Therefore, just as water retains no constant shape, so in warfare there are no constant conditions.

33. He who can modify his tactics in relation to his opponent and thereby succeed in winning, may be called a heaven-born captain.

34. The five elements (water, fire, wood, metal, earth) are not always equally

predominant; the four seasons make way for each other in turn. There are short days and long; the moon has its periods of waning and waxing.

CHAPTER 7.

MANEUVERING

1. Sun Tzu said: In war, the general receives his commands from the sovereign.

2. Having collected an army and concentrated his forces, he must blend and harmonize the different elements thereof before pitching his camp.

3. After that, comes tactical maneuvering, than which there is nothing more difficult. The difficulty of tactical maneuvering consists in turning the devious into the direct, and misfortune into gain.

4. Thus, to take a long and circuitous route, after enticing the enemy out of the way, and though starting after him, to contrive to reach the goal before him, shows knowledge of the artifice of DEVIATION.

5. Maneuvering with an army is advantageous; with an undisciplined multitude, most dangerous.

6. If you set a fully equipped army in march in order to snatch an advantage, the chances are that you will be too late. On the other hand, to detach a flying column for the purpose involves the sacrifice of its baggage and stores.

7. Thus, if you order your men to roll up their buff-coats, and make forced marches without halting day or night, covering double the usual distance at a stretch, doing a hundred LI in order to wrest an advantage, the leaders of all your three divisions will fall into the hands of the enemy.

8. The stronger men will be in front, the jaded ones will fall behind, and on this plan only

one-tenth of your army will reach its destination.

9. If you march fifty LI in order to outmaneuver the enemy, you will lose the leader of your first division, and only half your force will reach the goal.

10. If you march thirty LI with the same object, two-thirds of your army will arrive.

11. We may take it then that an army without its baggage train is lost; without provisions it is lost; without bases of supply it is lost.

12. We cannot enter into alliances until we are acquainted with the designs of our neighbors.

13. We are not fit to lead an army on the march unless we are familiar with the face of the country---its mountains and forests, its pitfalls and precipices, its marshes and swamps.

14. We shall be unable to turn natural advantage to account unless we make use of local guides.

15. In war, practice dissimulation, and you will succeed.

16. Whether to concentrate or to divide your troops, must be decided by circumstances.

17. Let your rapidity be that of the wind, your compactness that of the forest.

18. In raiding and plundering be like fire, in immovability like a mountain.

19. Let your plans be dark and impenetrable as night, and when you move, fall like a thunderbolt.

20. When you plunder a countryside, let the spoil be divided amongst your men; when you capture new territory, cut it up into allotments for the benefit of the soldiery.

21. Ponder and deliberate before you make a move.

22. He will conquer who has learnt the artifice of deviation. Such is the art of maneuvering.

23. The Book of Army Management says: On the field of battle, the spoken word does not carry far enough: hence the institution of gongs and drums. Nor can ordinary objects be seen clearly enough: hence the institution of banners and flags.

24. Gongs and drums, banners and flags, are means whereby the ears and eyes of the host may be focused on one particular point.

25. The host thus forming a single united body, is it impossible either for the brave to advance alone, or for the cowardly to retreat alone. This is the art of handling large masses of men.

26. In night-fighting, then, make much use of signal-fires and drums, and in fighting by day, of flags and banners, as a means of influencing the ears and eyes of your army.

27. A whole army may be robbed of its spirit; a commander-in-chief may be robbed of his presence of mind.
28. Now a soldier's spirit is keenest in the morning; by noonday it has begun to flag; and

in the evening, his mind is bent only on returning to camp.

29. A clever general, therefore, avoids an army when its spirit is keen, but attacks it when it is sluggish and inclined to return. This is the art of studying moods.

30. Disciplined and calm, to await the appearance of disorder and hubbub amongst the enemy:---this is the art of retaining self-possession.

31. To be near the goal while the enemy is still far from it, to wait at ease while the enemy is toiling and struggling, to be well-fed while the enemy is famished:---this is the art of husbanding one's strength.

32. To refrain from intercepting an enemy whose banners are in perfect order, to refrain from attacking an army drawn up in calm and confident array:---this is the art of studying circumstances.

33. It is a military axiom not to advance uphill against the enemy, nor to oppose him when he comes downhill.

34. Do not pursue an enemy who simulates flight; do not attack soldiers whose temper is keen.

35. Do not swallow bait offered by the enemy. Do not interfere with an army that is returning home.

36. When you surround an army, leave an outlet free. Do not press a desperate foe too hard.

37. Such is the art of warfare.

CHAPTER 8.

VARIATION IN TACTICS

1. Sun Tzu said: In war, the general receives his commands from the sovereign, collects his army and concentrates his forces.

2. When in difficult country, do not encamp. In country where high roads intersect, join hands with your allies. Do not linger in dangerously isolated positions. In hemmed-in situations, you must resort to stratagem. In desperate position, you must fight.

3. There are roads which must not be followed, armies which must be not attacked, towns which must not be besieged, positions

which must not be contested, commands of the sovereign which must not be obeyed.

4. The general who thoroughly understands the advantages that accompany variation of tactics knows how to handle his troops.

5. The general who does not understand these, may be well acquainted with the configuration of the country, yet he will not be able to turn his knowledge to practical account.

6. So, the student of war who is unversed in the art of war of varying his plans, even though he be acquainted with the Five Advantages, will fail to make the best use of his men.

7. Hence in the wise leader's plans, considerations of advantage and of disadvantage will be blended together.

8. If our expectation of advantage be tempered in this way, we may succeed in accomplishing the essential part of our schemes.

9. If, on the other hand, in the midst of difficulties we are always ready to seize an advantage, we may extricate ourselves from misfortune.

10. Reduce the hostile chiefs by inflicting damage on them; and make trouble for them, and keep them constantly engaged; hold out specious allurements, and make them rush to any given point.

11. The art of war teaches us to rely not on the likelihood of the enemy's not coming, but on our own readiness to receive him; not on the chance of his not attacking, but rather on the fact that we have made our position unassailable.

12. There are five dangerous faults which may affect a general: (1) Recklessness, which leads to destruction; (2) cowardice, which leads to capture; (3) a hasty temper, which can be provoked by insults; (4) a delicacy of honor which is sensitive to shame; (5) over-solicitude for his men, which exposes him to worry and trouble.

13. These are the five besetting sins of a general, ruinous to the conduct of war.

14. When an army is overthrown and its leader slain, the cause will surely be found among these five dangerous faults. Let them be a subject of meditation.

CHAPTER 9.

THE ARMY ON THE MARCH

1. Sun Tzu said: We come now to the question of encamping the army, and observing signs of the enemy. Pass quickly over mountains, and keep in the neighborhood of valleys.

2. Camp in high places, facing the sun. Do not climb heights in order to fight. So much for mountain warfare.

3. After crossing a river, you should get far away from it.

4. When an invading force crosses a river in its onward march, do not advance to meet it in mid-stream. It will be best to let half the army get across, and then deliver your attack.

5. If you are anxious to fight, you should not go to meet the invader near a river which he has to cross.

6. Moor your craft higher up than the enemy, and facing the sun. Do not move up-stream to meet the enemy. So much for river warfare.

7. In crossing salt-marshes, your sole concern should be to get over them quickly, without any delay.

8. If forced to fight in a salt-marsh, you should have water and grass near you, and get your back to a clump of trees. So much for operations in salt-marches.

9. In dry, level country, take up an easily accessible position with rising ground to your right and on your rear, so that the danger may be in front, and safety lie behind. So much for campaigning in flat country.

10. These are the four useful branches of military knowledge which enabled the Yellow Emperor to vanquish four several sovereigns.

11. All armies prefer high ground to low. and sunny places to dark.

12. If you are careful of your men, and camp on hard ground, the army will be free from disease of every kind, and this will spell victory.

13. When you come to a hill or a bank, occupy the sunny side, with the slope on your right rear. Thus you will at once act for the benefit of your soldiers and utilize the natural advantages of the ground.

14. When, in consequence of heavy rains up-country, a river which you wish to ford is swollen and flecked with foam, you must wait until it subsides.

15. Country in which there are precipitous cliffs with torrents running between, deep natural hollows, confined places, tangled thickets, quagmires and crevasses, should be

left with all possible speed and not approached.

16. While we keep away from such places, we should get the enemy to approach them; while we face them, we should let the enemy have them on his rear.

17. If in the neighborhood of your camp there should be any hilly country, ponds surrounded by aquatic grass, hollow basins filled with reeds, or woods with thick undergrowth, they must be carefully routed out and searched; for these are places where men in ambush or insidious spies are likely to be lurking.

18. When the enemy is close at hand and remains quiet, he is relying on the natural strength of his position.

19. When he keeps aloof and tries to provoke a battle, he is anxious for the other side to advance.

20. If his place of encampment is easy of access, he is tendering a bait.

21. Movement amongst the trees of a forest shows that the enemy is advancing. The appearance of a number of screens in the midst of thick grass means that the enemy wants to make us suspicious.

22. The rising of birds in their flight is the sign of an ambuscade. Startled beasts indicate that a sudden attack is coming.

23. When there is dust rising in a high column, it is the sign of chariots advancing; when the dust is low, but spread over a wide area, it betokens the approach of infantry. When it branches out in different directions, it shows that parties have been sent to collect firewood. A few clouds of dust moving to and fro signify that the army is encamping.

24. Humble words and increased preparations are signs that the enemy is about to advance. Violent language and driving forward as if to the attack are signs that he will retreat.

25. When the light chariots come out first and take up a position on the wings, it is a sign that the enemy is forming for battle.

26. Peace proposals unaccompanied by a sworn covenant indicate a plot.

27. When there is much running about and the soldiers fall into rank, it means that the critical moment has come.

28. When some are seen advancing and some retreating, it is a lure.

29. When the soldiers stand leaning on their spears, they are faint from want of food.

30. If those who are sent to draw water begin by drinking themselves, the army is suffering from thirst.

31. If the enemy sees an advantage to be gained and makes no effort to secure it, the soldiers are exhausted.

32. If birds gather on any spot, it is unoccupied. Clamor by night betokens nervousness.

33. If there is disturbance in the camp, the general's authority is weak. If the banners and

flags are shifted about, sedition is afoot. If the officers are angry, it means that the men are weary.

34. When an army feeds its horses with grain and kills its cattle for food, and when the men do not hang their cooking-pots over the camp fires, showing that they will not return to their tents, you may know that they are determined to fight to the death.

35. The sight of men whispering together in small knots or speaking in subdued tones points to disaffection amongst the rank and file.

36. Too frequent rewards signify that the enemy is at the end of his resources; too many punishments betray a condition of dire distress.

37. To begin by bluster, but afterwards to take fright at the enemy's numbers, shows a supreme lack of intelligence.

38. When envoys are sent with compliments in their mouths, it is a sign that the enemy wishes for a truce.

39. If the enemy's troops march up angrily and remain facing ours for a long time without either joining battle or taking themselves off again, the situation is one that demands great vigilance and circumspection.

40. If our troops are no more in number than the enemy, that is amply sufficient; it only means that no direct attack can be made. What we can do is simply to concentrate all our available strength, keep a close watch on the enemy, and obtain reinforcements.

41. He who exercises no forethought but makes light of his opponents is sure to be captured by them.

42. If soldiers are punished before they have grown attached to you, they will not prove submissive; and, unless submissive, then will be practically useless. If, when the soldiers have become attached to you, punishments are not enforced, they will still be useless.

43. Therefore soldiers must be treated in the first instance with humanity, but kept under control by means of iron discipline. This is a certain road to victory.

44. If in training soldiers commands are habitually enforced, the army will be well-disciplined; if not, its discipline will be bad.

45. If a general shows confidence in his men but always insists on his orders being obeyed, the gain will be mutual.

CHAPTER 10.

TERRAIN

1. Sun Tzu said: We may distinguish six kinds of terrain, to wit: (1) Accessible ground; (2) entangling ground; (3) temporizing ground; (4) narrow passes; (5) precipitous heights; (6) positions at a great distance from the enemy.

2. Ground which can be freely traversed by both sides is called ACCESSIBLE.

3. With regard to ground of this nature, be before the enemy in occupying the raised and sunny spots, and carefully guard your line of supplies. Then you will be able to fight with advantage.

4. Ground which can be abandoned but is hard to re-occupy is called ENTANGLING.

5. From a position of this sort, if the enemy is unprepared, you may sally forth and defeat him. But if the enemy is prepared for your coming, and you fail to defeat him, then, return being impossible, disaster will ensue.

6. When the position is such that neither side will gain by making the first move, it is called TEMPORIZING ground.

7. In a position of this sort, even though the enemy should offer us an attractive bait, it will be advisable not to stir forth, but rather to retreat, thus enticing the enemy in his turn; then, when part of his army has come out, we may deliver our attack with advantage.

8. With regard to NARROW PASSES, if you can occupy them first, let them be strongly garrisoned and await the advent of the enemy.

9. Should the army forestall you in occupying a pass, do not go after him if the pass is fully garrisoned, but only if it is weakly garrisoned.

10. With regard to PRECIPITOUS HEIGHTS, if you are beforehand with your adversary, you should occupy the raised and sunny spots, and there wait for him to come up.

11. If the enemy has occupied them before you, do not follow him, but retreat and try to entice him away.

12. If you are situated at a great distance from the enemy, and the strength of the two armies is equal, it is not easy to provoke a battle, and fighting will be to your disadvantage.

13. These six are the principles connected with Earth. The general who has attained a responsible post must be careful to study them.

14. Now an army is exposed to six several calamities, not arising from natural causes, but from faults for which the general is responsible. These are: (1) Flight; (2) insubordination; (3) collapse; (4) ruin; (5) disorganization; (6) rout.

15. Other conditions being equal, if one force is hurled against another ten times its size, the result will be the FLIGHT of the former.

16. When the common soldiers are too strong and their officers too weak, the result is INSUBORDINATION. When the officers are too strong and the common soldiers too weak, the result is COLLAPSE.

17. When the higher officers are angry and insubordinate, and on meeting the enemy give battle on their own account from a feeling of resentment, before the commander-in-chief can tell whether or no he is in a position to fight, the result is RUIN.

18. When the general is weak and without authority; when his orders are not clear and distinct; when there are no fixes duties assigned to officers and men, and the ranks are formed in a slovenly haphazard manner, the result is utter DISORGANIZATION.

19. When a general, unable to estimate the enemy's strength, allows an inferior force to engage a larger one, or hurls a weak

detachment against a powerful one, and neglects to place picked soldiers in the front rank, the result must be ROUT.

20. These are six ways of courting defeat, which must be carefully noted by the general who has attained a responsible post.

21. The natural formation of the country is the soldier's best ally; but a power of estimating the adversary, of controlling the forces of victory, and of shrewdly calculating difficulties, dangers and distances, constitutes the test of a great general.

22. He who knows these things, and in fighting puts his knowledge into practice, will win his battles. He who knows them not, nor practices them, will surely be defeated.

23. If fighting is sure to result in victory, then you must fight, even though the ruler forbid it; if fighting will not result in victory, then you must not fight even at the ruler's bidding.

24. The general who advances without coveting fame and retreats without fearing

disgrace, whose only thought is to protect his country and do good service for his sovereign, is the jewel of the kingdom.

25. Regard your soldiers as your children, and they will follow you into the deepest valleys; look upon them as your own beloved sons, and they will stand by you even unto death.

26. If, however, you are indulgent, but unable to make your authority felt; kind-hearted, but unable to enforce your commands; and incapable, moreover, of quelling disorder: then your soldiers must be likened to spoilt children; they are useless for any practical purpose.

27. If we know that our own men are in a condition to attack, but are unaware that the enemy is not open to attack, we have gone only halfway towards victory.

28. If we know that the enemy is open to attack, but are unaware that our own men are not in a condition to attack, we have gone only halfway towards victory.

29. If we know that the enemy is open to attack, and also know that our men are in a condition to attack, but are unaware that the nature of the ground makes fighting impracticable, we have still gone only halfway towards victory.

30. Hence the experienced soldier, once in motion, is never bewildered; once he has broken camp, he is never at a loss.

31. Hence the saying: If you know the enemy and know yourself, your victory will not stand in doubt; if you know Heaven and know Earth, you may make your victory complete.

CHAPTER 11.

THE NINE SITUATIONS

1. Sun Tzu said: The art of war recognizes nine varieties of ground: (1) Dispersive ground; (2) facile ground; (3) contentious ground; (4) open ground; (5) ground of intersecting highways; (6) serious ground; (7) difficult ground; (8) hemmed-in ground; (9) desperate ground.

2. When a chieftain is fighting in his own territory, it is dispersive ground.

3. When he has penetrated into hostile territory, but to no great distance, it is facile ground.

4. Ground the possession of which imports great advantage to either side, is contentious ground.

5. Ground on which each side has liberty of movement is open ground.

6. Ground which forms the key to three contiguous states, so that he who occupies it first has most of the Empire at his command, is a ground of intersecting highways.

7. When an army has penetrated into the heart of a hostile country, leaving a number of fortified cities in its rear, it is serious ground.

8. Mountain forests, rugged steeps, marshes and fens---all country that is hard to traverse: this is difficult ground.

9. Ground which is reached through narrow gorges, and from which we can only retire by tortuous paths, so that a small number of the enemy would suffice to crush a large body of our men: this is hemmed in ground.

10. Ground on which we can only be saved from destruction by fighting without delay, is desperate ground.

11. On dispersive ground, therefore, fight not. On facile ground, halt not. On contentious ground, attack not.

12. On open ground, do not try to block the enemy's way. On the ground of intersecting highways, join hands with your allies.

13. On serious ground, gather in plunder. In difficult ground, keep steadily on the march.

14. On hemmed-in ground, resort to stratagem. On desperate ground, fight.

15. Those who were called skillful leaders of old knew how to drive a wedge between the enemy's front and rear; to prevent co-operation between his large and small divisions; to hinder the good troops from rescuing the bad, the officers from rallying their men.

16. When the enemy's men were united, they managed to keep them in disorder.

17. When it was to their advantage, they made a forward move; when otherwise, they stopped still.

18. If asked how to cope with a great host of the enemy in orderly array and on the point of marching to the attack, I should say: "Begin by seizing something which your opponent holds dear; then he will be amenable to your will."

19. Rapidity is the essence of war: take advantage of the enemy's unreadiness, make your way by unexpected routes, and attack unguarded spots.

20. The following are the principles to be observed by an invading force: The further you penetrate into a country, the greater will be the solidarity of your troops, and thus the defenders will not prevail against you.

21. Make forays in fertile country in order to supply your army with food.

22. Carefully study the well-being of your men, and do not overtax them. Concentrate your energy and hoard your strength. Keep your army continually on the move, and devise unfathomable plans.

23. Throw your soldiers into positions whence there is no escape, and they will prefer death to flight. If they will face death, there is nothing they may not achieve. Officers and men alike will put forth their uttermost strength.

24. Soldiers when in desperate straits lose the sense of fear. If there is no place of refuge, they will stand firm. If they are in hostile country, they will show a stubborn front. If there is no help for it, they will fight hard.

25. Thus, without waiting to be marshaled, the soldiers will be constantly on the qui vive; without waiting to be asked, they will do your will; without restrictions, they will be faithful; without giving orders, they can be trusted.

26. Prohibit the taking of omens, and do away with superstitious doubts. Then, until death itself comes, no calamity need be feared.

27. If our soldiers are not overburdened with money, it is not because they have a distaste for riches; if their lives are not unduly long, it is not because they are disinclined to longevity.

28. On the day they are ordered out to battle, your soldiers may weep, those sitting up bedewing their garments, and those lying down letting the tears run down their cheeks. But let them once be brought to bay, and they will display the courage of a Chu or a Kuei.

29. The skillful tactician may be likened to the SHUAI-JAN. Now the SHUAI-JAN is a snake that is found in the Ch`ang mountains. Strike at its head, and you will be attacked by its tail; strike at its tail, and you will be attacked by its head; strike at its middle, and you will be attacked by head and tail both.

30. Asked if an army can be made to imitate the SHUAI-JAN, I should answer, Yes. For

the men of Wu and the men of Yueh are enemies; yet if they are crossing a river in the same boat and are caught by a storm, they will come to each other's assistance just as the left hand helps the right.

31. Hence it is not enough to put one's trust in the tethering of horses, and the burying of chariot wheels in the ground

32. The principle on which to manage an army is to set up one standard of courage which all must reach.

33. How to make the best of both strong and weak---that is a question involving the proper use of ground.

34. Thus the skillful general conducts his army just as though he were leading a single man, willy-nilly, by the hand.

35. It is the business of a general to be quiet and thus ensure secrecy; upright and just, and thus maintain order.

36. He must be able to mystify his officers and men by false reports and appearances, and thus keep them in total ignorance.

37. By altering his arrangements and changing his plans, he keeps the enemy without definite knowledge. By shifting his camp and taking circuitous routes, he prevents the enemy from anticipating his purpose.

38. At the critical moment, the leader of an army acts like one who has climbed up a height and then kicks away the ladder behind him. He carries his men deep into hostile territory before he shows his hand.
39. He burns his boats and breaks his cooking-pots; like a shepherd driving a flock of sheep, he drives his men this way and that, and nothing knows whither he is going.

40. To muster his host and bring it into danger:---this may be termed the business of the general.

41. The different measures suited to the nine varieties of ground; the expediency of aggressive or defensive tactics; and the

fundamental laws of human nature: these are things that must most certainly be studied.

42. When invading hostile territory, the general principle is, that penetrating deeply brings cohesion; penetrating but a short way means dispersion.

43. When you leave your own country behind, and take your army across neighborhood territory, you find yourself on critical ground. When there are means of communication on all four sides, the ground is one of intersecting highways.

44. When you penetrate deeply into a country, it is serious ground. When you penetrate but a little way, it is facile ground.

45. When you have the enemy's strongholds on your rear, and narrow passes in front, it is hemmed-in ground. When there is no place of refuge at all, it is desperate ground.
46. Therefore, on dispersive ground, I would inspire my men with unity of purpose. On facile ground, I would see that there is close connection between all parts of my army.

47. On contentious ground, I would hurry up my rear.

48. On open ground, I would keep a vigilant eye on my defenses. On ground of intersecting highways, I would consolidate my alliances.

49. On serious ground, I would try to ensure a continuous stream of supplies. On difficult ground, I would keep pushing on along the road.

50. On hemmed-in ground, I would block any way of retreat. On desperate ground, I would proclaim to my soldiers the hopelessness of saving their lives.

51. For it is the soldier's disposition to offer an obstinate resistance when surrounded, to fight hard when he cannot help himself, and to obey promptly when he has fallen into danger.

52. We cannot enter into alliance with neighboring princes until we are acquainted with their designs. We are not fit to lead an

army on the march unless we are familiar with the face of the country---its mountains and forests, its pitfalls and precipices, its marshes and swamps. We shall be unable to turn natural advantages to account unless we make use of local guides.

53. To be ignored of any one of the following four or five principles does not befit a warlike prince.

54. When a warlike prince attacks a powerful state, his generalship shows itself in preventing the concentration of the enemy's forces. He overawes his opponents, and their allies are prevented from joining against him.

55. Hence he does not strive to ally himself with all and sundry, nor does he foster the power of other states. He carries out his own secret designs, keeping his antagonists in awe. Thus he is able to capture their cities and overthrow their kingdoms.

56. Bestow rewards without regard to rule, issue orders without regard to previous arrangements; and you will be able to handle a

whole army as though you had to do with but a single man.

57. Confront your soldiers with the deed itself; never let them know your design. When the outlook is bright, bring it before their eyes; but tell them nothing when the situation is gloomy.

58. Place your army in deadly peril, and it will survive; plunge it into desperate straits, and it will come off in safety.

59. For it is precisely when a force has fallen into harm's way that is capable of striking a blow for victory.

60. Success in warfare is gained by carefully accommodating ourselves to the enemy's purpose.

61. By persistently hanging on the enemy's flank, we shall succeed in the long run in killing the commander-in-chief.

62. This is called ability to accomplish a thing by sheer cunning.

63. On the day that you take up your command, block the frontier passes, destroy the official tallies, and stop the passage of all emissaries.

64. Be stern in the council-chamber, so that you may control the situation.

65. If the enemy leaves a door open, you must rush in.

66. Forestall your opponent by seizing what he holds dear, and subtly contrive to time his arrival on the ground.

67. Walk in the path defined by rule, and accommodate yourself to the enemy until you can fight a decisive battle.

68. At first, then, exhibit the coyness of a maiden, until the enemy gives you an opening; afterwards emulate the rapidity of a running hare, and it will be too late for the enemy to oppose you.

CHAPTER 12.

THE ATTACK BY FIRE

1. Sun Tzu said: There are five ways of attacking with fire. The first is to burn soldiers in their camp; the second is to burn stores; the third is to burn baggage trains; the fourth is to burn arsenals and magazines; the fifth is to hurl dropping fire amongst the enemy.

2. In order to carry out an attack, we must have means available. the material for raising fire should always be kept in readiness.

3. There is a proper season for making attacks with fire, and special days for starting a conflagration.

4. The proper season is when the weather is very dry; the special days are those when the moon is in the constellations of the Sieve, the Wall, the Wing or the Cross-bar; for these four are all days of rising wind.

5. In attacking with fire, one should be prepared to meet five possible developments:

6. (1) When fire breaks out inside to enemy's camp, respond at once with an attack from without.

7. (2) If there is an outbreak of fire, but the enemy's soldiers remain quiet, bide your time and do not attack.

8. (3) When the force of the flames has reached its height, follow it up with an attack, if that is practicable; if not, stay where you are.

9. (4) If it is possible to make an assault with fire from without, do not wait for it to break out within, but deliver your attack at a favorable moment.

10. (5) When you start a fire, be to windward of it. Do not attack from the leeward.

11. A wind that rises in the daytime lasts long, but a night breeze soon falls.

12. In every army, the five developments connected with fire must be known, the movements of the stars calculated, and a watch kept for the proper days.

13. Hence those who use fire as an aid to the attack show intelligence; those who use water as an aid to the attack gain an accession of strength.

14. By means of water, an enemy may be intercepted, but not robbed of all his belongings.

15. Unhappy is the fate of one who tries to win his battles and succeed in his attacks without cultivating the spirit of enterprise; for the result is waste of time and general stagnation.

16. Hence the saying: The enlightened ruler lays his plans well ahead; the good general cultivates his resources.

17. Move not unless you see an advantage; use not your troops unless there is something to be gained; fight not unless the position is critical.

18. No ruler should put troops into the field merely to gratify his own spleen; no general should fight a battle simply out of pique.

19. If it is to your advantage, make a forward move; if not, stay where you are.

20. Anger may in time change to gladness; vexation may be succeeded by content.

21. But a kingdom that has once been destroyed can never come again into being; nor can the dead ever be brought back to life.

22. Hence the enlightened ruler is heedful, and the good general full of caution. This is the way to keep a country at peace and an army intact.

CHAPTER 13.

THE USE OF SPIES

1. Sun Tzu said: Raising a host of a hundred thousand men and marching them great distances entails heavy loss on the people and a drain on the resources of the State. The daily expenditure will amount to a thousand ounces of silver. There will be commotion at home and abroad, and men will drop down exhausted on the highways. As many as seven hundred thousand families will be impeded in their labor.

2. Hostile armies may face each other for years, striving for the victory which is decided in a single day. This being so, to remain in ignorance of the enemy's condition simply because one grudges the outlay of a hundred ounces of silver in honors and emoluments, is the height of inhumanity.

3. One who acts thus is no leader of men, no present help to his sovereign, no master of victory.

4. Thus, what enables the wise sovereign and the good general to strike and conquer, and achieve things beyond the reach of ordinary men, is FOREKNOWLEDGE.

5. Now this foreknowledge cannot be elicited from spirits; it cannot be obtained inductively from experience, nor by any deductive calculation.

6. Knowledge of the enemy's dispositions can only be obtained from other men.

7. Hence the use of spies, of whom there are five classes: (1) Local spies; (2) inward spies;

(3) converted spies; (4) doomed spies; (5) surviving spies.

8. When these five kinds of spy are all at work, none can discover the secret system. This is called "divine manipulation of the threads." It is the sovereign's most precious faculty.

9. Having LOCAL SPIES means employing the services of the inhabitants of a district.

10. Having INWARD SPIES, making use of officials of the enemy.

11. Having CONVERTED SPIES, getting hold of the enemy's spies and using them for our own purposes.

12. Having DOOMED SPIES, doing certain things openly for purposes of deception, and allowing our spies to know of them and report them to the enemy.

13. SURVIVING SPIES, finally, are those who bring back news from the enemy's camp.

14. Hence it is that which none in the whole army are more intimate relations to be maintained than with spies. None should be more liberally rewarded. In no other business should greater secrecy be preserved.

15. Spies cannot be usefully employed without a certain intuitive sagacity.

16. They cannot be properly managed without benevolence and straightforwardness.

17. Without subtle ingenuity of mind, one cannot make certain of the truth of their reports.

18. Be subtle! be subtle! and use your spies for every kind of business.

19. If a secret piece of news is divulged by a spy before the time is ripe, he must be put to death together with the man to whom the secret was told.

20. Whether the object be to crush an army, to storm a city, or to assassinate an individual, it is always necessary to begin by finding out

the names of the attendants, the aides-de-camp, and door-keepers and sentries of the general in command. Our spies must be commissioned to ascertain these.

21. The enemy's spies who have come to spy on us must be sought out, tempted with bribes, led away and comfortably housed. Thus they will become converted spies and available for our service.

22. It is through the information brought by the converted spy that we are able to acquire and employ local and inward spies.

23. It is owing to his information, again, that we can cause the doomed spy to carry false tidings to the enemy.

24. Lastly, it is by his information that the surviving spy can be used on appointed occasions.

25. The end and aim of spying in all its five varieties is knowledge of the enemy; and this knowledge can only be derived, in the first instance, from the converted spy. Hence it is

essential that the converted spy be treated with the utmost liberality.

26. Of old, the rise of the Yin dynasty was due to I Chih who had served under the Hsia. Likewise, the rise of the Chou dynasty was due to Lu Ya who had served under the Yin.

27. Hence it is only the enlightened ruler and the wise general who will use the highest intelligence of the army for purposes of spying and thereby they achieve great results. Spies are a most important element in water, because on them depends an army's ability to move.